MEDIEVAL ORNAMENT

950 Illustrations

Karl Alexander von Heideloff

DOVER PUBLICATIONS, INC.

NEW YORK

Bibliographical Note

This Dover edition, first published in 1995, contains all 200 plates from the two volumes of *Carl Heideloff's Ornamentik des Mittelalters: 200 Kupfertafeln mit erklärendem Text*, as published by C. Geiger's Verlag, Nuremberg, n.d. (see Publisher's Note for further bibliographical details). The Publisher's Note was written specially for the present edition, as were the new English captions, abridged translations of the original German explanatory text. The plates reproduced here are courtesy of Cornell University Fine Arts Library.

Library of Congress Cataloging-in-Publication Data

Heideloff, Carl Alexander von, 1788–1865.
[Ornamentik des Mittelalters. English. Selections]
Medieval ornament / Karl Alexander von Heideloff.
p. cm.—(Dover pictorial archive series)
"This Dover edition, first published in 1995, contains all 200 plates from the two volumes of Carl Heideloff's Ornamentik des Mittelalters : 200 Kupfertafeln mit erklärendem Text, as published by G. Geiger's Verlag, Nuremberg, n.d."—T.p. verso.
ISBN 0-486-28578-2 (pbk.)
1. Decoration and ornament, Medieval. 2. Decoration and ornament, Architectural, 3. Architecture, Medieval. I. Title. II. Series.
NA3390.H4213 1995
729′.094′0902—dc20
95-21220
CIP

Manufactured in the United States of America
Dover Publications, Inc., 31 East 2nd Street, Mineola, N.Y. 11501

Publisher's Note

Karl (or Carl) Alexander von Heideloff (1789–1865) was principally an architect, although his talents also included painting, sculpture and engraving. As an architect he was chiefly involved, from at least 1816, with the restoration of Romanesque and Gothic buildings in Germany and in the design of new buildings in the Neo-Gothic style that was popular there throughout the nineteenth century. (Since the 1770s the Gothic style had been considered peculiarly, nationalistically German, and the Romantics had celebrated things medieval as a patriotic contrast to the Italian- and French-inspired Baroque, Rococo and Neo-Classical styles that had immediately preceded.) Heideloff's center of operations was Nuremberg, where for some three decades he was curator of municipal art monuments and instructor at the Polytechnic.

Among Heideloff's numerous publications, the present collection of 200 copperplate engravings (apparently all drawn by him, although engraved by several hands) is outstanding, but rather hard to date (all encyclopedia references we have seen are obviously wrong if the dates engraved on the plates are to be trusted). The source of this Dover edition is a two-volume set titled *Carl Heideloffs Ornamentik des Mittelalters: 200 Kupfertafeln mit erklärendem Text* [Carl Heideloff's Ornament of the Middle Ages: 200 Copperplates with Explanatory Text], published in Nuremberg by C. Geiger without a printed date. There is no introductory text, only several pages of descriptions of the plates, which were obviously written by someone other than Heideloff, and which read in several places as though he were already dead (although he died ten years later than the last date engraved on any plate).

From the numbering of the plates (which corresponds to the printed descriptions), they were originally issued in 25 groups of eight (Heft I, Pl. 1–8, through Heft XXV, Pl. 1–8); in the present edition, they have been renumbered consecutively from 1 through 200. The engraved dates that appear sporadically on the plates indicate that, with a handful of slight anomalies, the plates are numbered in the sequence of their being engraved; they also indicate lapses of time here and there. Plate 5 (the Dover numbers are here used) is dated 1837; Plate 13 is dated 1838; the dates 1841 and 1842 (with some jumpiness) appear between Plates 25 and 37; the date 1843 appears between Plates 47 and 61; 1844 appears between Plates 72 and 83; 1845 appears on Plates 97 and 101; 1846 appears between Plates 105 and 121; 1847, between Plates 123 and 137; 1850, between 146 and 167; 1851, between Plates 171 and 179; 1852, between Plates 180 and 187; 1854 and 1855 (with jumpiness), between Plates 193 and 200.

The plates are a rich resource of rare ornamental elements of (now largely destroyed) buildings and furniture, chiefly ecclesiastical, principally from Germany (and, within Germany, mainly from the south, the present-day Länder of Baden-Württemberg and Bavaria, where Heideloff was most active); there is an occasional foray into Austria, Switzerland and France. Many of the plates record restoration or original work by Heideloff himself. The new English captions are based on the German plate descriptions in the Geiger publication, which have been somewhat abridged for the present edition. The spellings of small localities that could not be checked are generally given as in the original, despite a few apparent inconsistencies.

1. Four Romanesque column capitals from St. Sebald's, Nuremberg. With details of profiling.

2. *a, b, d, e:* Four Romanesque column capitals from St. Sebald's, Nuremberg. *c, f, h:*
Romanesque consoles from the same church. With side and profile views.

3. *a:* Painted Romanesque frieze in the Holy Cross Monastery near Meissen, Saxony. *b:* Ornament of the keystone of a cruciform vault, St. Sebald's, Nuremberg. *c:* Ornament over a church door in Nossen, Saxony. *d–g:* Profiles of various elements of columns.

4. *a:* Ornament on the portal of the Burgraves' Chapel in the Heilsbronn monastery. *b, c:* Keystones of vaults, St. Sebald's, Nuremberg. *d:* Painted Romanesque ornament in St. Peter's choir of Bamberg Cathedral.

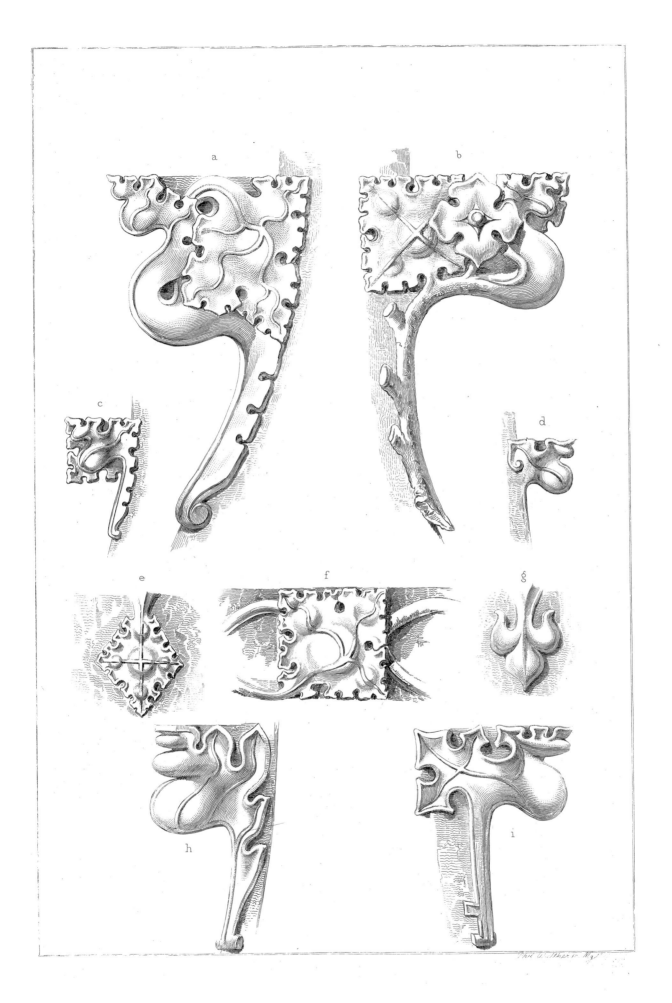

5. Gothic architectural ornaments. *a:* Crocket from a church in Rouen. *b, f:* Crocket and leaf from Notre-Dame, Paris. *c, d:* Crockets from St. Lawrence's, Nuremberg. *e, g:* From the organ of St. Sebald's, Nuremberg. *h, i:* Crockets from choir stalls in St. Lawrence's, Nuremberg (15th century).

a

b

c

d

6. Ornament from the bridal coach of Princess Agnes of Hesse, wife of Duke Johann
Friedrich of Saxe-Coburg, 1555; carved wood (very low relief), gilded.

7. Ornament from the bridal coach of Princess Agnes of Hesse.

8. Bishop's crosier and cross, carved and gilded wood, from two figures in an altarpiece, ascribed to Veit Stoss, in the Germanisches Museum, Nuremberg.

a

b

c

d   *e*

9. Romanesque ornaments. *a–c:* Friezes on the exterior of the former diocese church in Ellwangen, Württemberg. *d:* Capital from St. Germain Abbey, Paris. *e:* Capital from the Ottmar Chapel in the Nuremberg citadel.

a

b

c

d

Ph. Walther sc.

10. Romanesque ornament. *a:* Pillar capital from the ruins of the Benedictine monastery at Hirschau, Württemberg. *b:* Pillar capital from the Benedictine abbey at Murrhard. *c:* Column capital from St. Sebald's, Nuremberg. *d:* Column capital from the monastery church of the Holy Grave, Denkendorf, Württemberg.

11. *a:* Late Gothic ornament from the leather binding of a missal in the church at Erlbach, Bavaria. *b:* Gothic leaf from the metal frame of the painting on the Mary Altar at Rottweil in the Black Forest. *c:* Late Gothic sheet-iron ornament from the lock of the former Tallow House, Nuremberg. *d:* Late Gothic keyplate from a residence, Nuremberg. *e, g, h, i:* Late Gothic iron rosettes from doors of Nuremberg residences. *f:* Keystone of an arch in the Gothic church of St. Jobst near Nuremberg.

12. *a:* Embroidered edges of an altarcloth, St. Lawrence's, Nuremberg. *b–d:* Pewter crown from a statue of the Virgin in St. Lawrence's, Nuremberg; with details. *e:* Sheet-iron rosette on the knocker of the sacristy door, St. Lawrence's, Nuremberg.

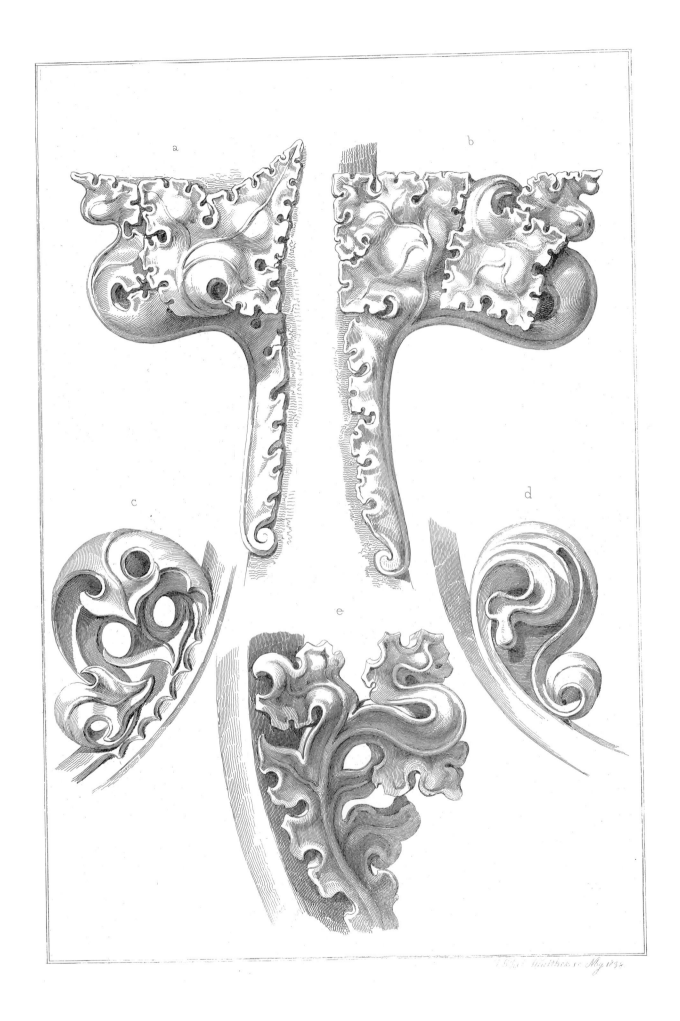

13. *a, b:* Crockets from a church in Rouen. *c–e:* Wooden crockets from choir stalls in St. Lawrence's, Nuremberg.

14. *a:* Low-relief wooden carvings from the courtyard of a house in Nuremberg. *b, d:* Console and ornament from the late 15th-century altarpiece (carved and gilded wood) in the Holy Cross Chapel near Nuremberg. *c:* Arms of the Haller von Hallerstein family in the Holy Cross Chapel.

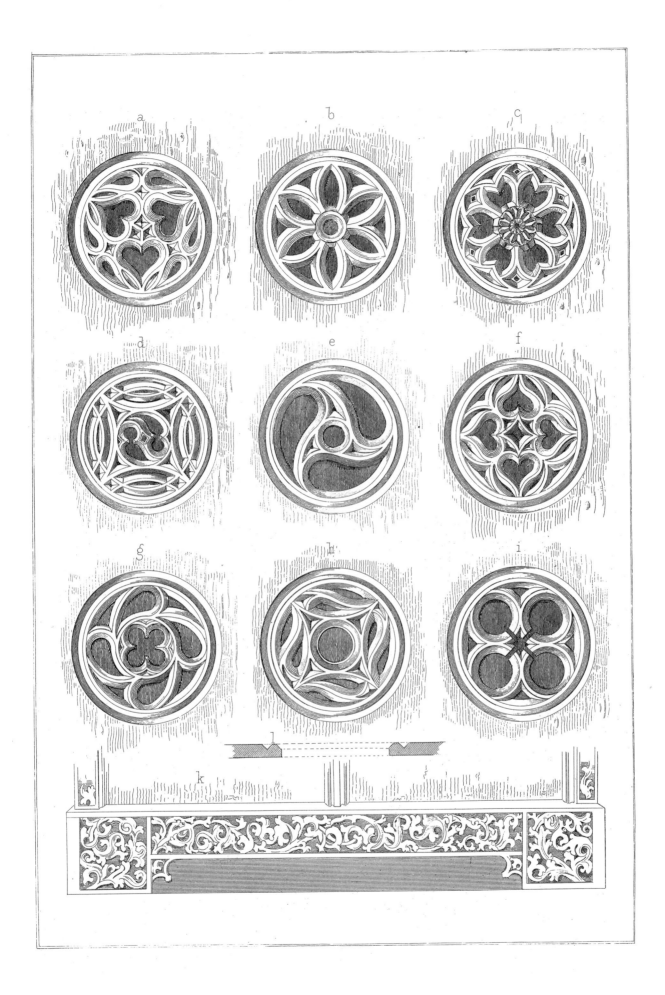

15. *a–i:* Nine late Gothic carved-wood rosettes from the choir stalls of the former monastery church of St. Clara, Nuremberg. *k:* Foot of a now destroyed late Gothic armoire in the church of the Franciscan monastery, Nuremberg. *l:* Profile of the above rosettes.

16. Foot of the sacrament house in St. Michael's, Fürth.

17. *a–d:* Corbels on the so-called Pagans' Tower in the Nuremberg citadel. *e:* Pillar pinnacle in the choir of the monastery church, Heilsbronn, Bavaria. *f:* Romanesque ornament from the tympanum of the portal to the churchyard chapel, Heilsbronn.

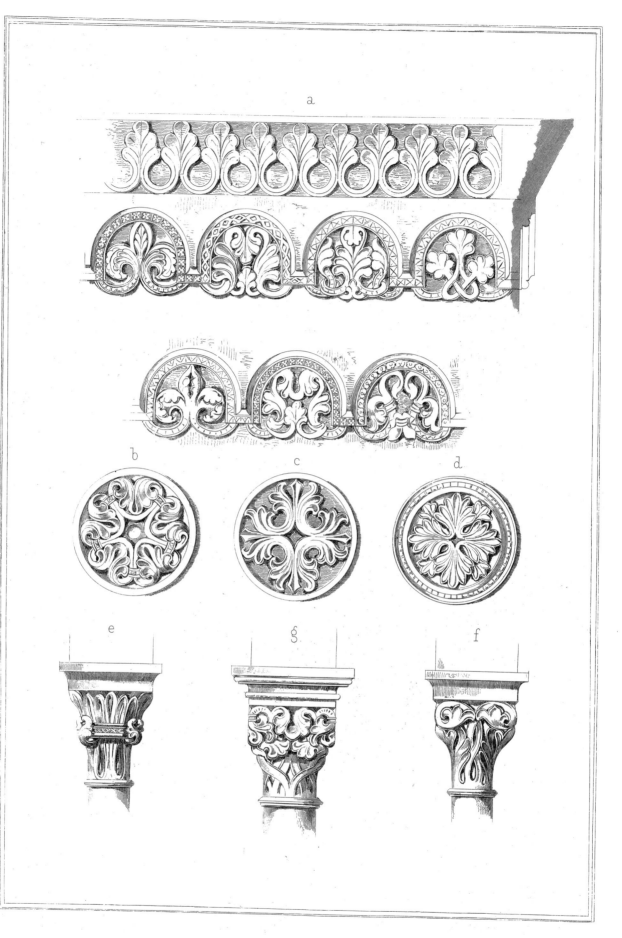

18. *a:* Romanesque frieze in the St. Walderich Chapel of the Murrhard monastery. *b:* Romanesque rosette from the Bamberg Cathedral. *c:* Rosette from the choir of St. Clara's, Nuremberg. *d:* Rosette from the monastery church, Heilsbronn, Bavaria. *e, f:* Column capitals from the chapel of Veste Coburg. *g:* Column capital from St. Sebald's, Nuremberg.

a

b

c

d

e

bel. Grunewald sc

19. *a–d:* Portal friezes from the St. Walderich Chapel of the Murrhard monastery. *e:* Six corbels from St. Sebald's, Nuremberg.

20. *a:* Late Gothic corbel in the choir of St. Lawrence's, Nuremberg. *b–g:* Various wood ornaments on the choir stalls of St. Lawrence's, Nuremberg.

21. *a:* Late Gothic lock plate from the Bebenhaus hospice in Tübingen. *b:* Late Gothic iron handle on an armoire in the church at Market Erlbach. *c:* Iron ornament from the old St. Lawrence parsonage in Nuremberg. *d:* Late Gothic iron rosette from the door of the Holy Cross Chapel near Nuremberg. *e:* Late Gothic iron rosette from a Nuremberg residence. *f:* Wooden crocket on a choir stall of St. George's, Tübingen. *g:* Wooden crocket on a choir stall of the former hospital church in Stuttgart. *h:* Late Gothic carved-wood ornaments from the Bebenhausen monastery.

22. Late Gothic carved-wood ornaments on the choir stalls of St. George's, Tübingen.

23. Baptismal font from St. Mary's, Reutlingen, with details.

24. Late Gothic sacrament house from the monastery church in Offenhausen.

Phil Walther s. lig. 1842.

25. *a, b:* Capitals from the church of the Cistercian monastery at Lilienfeld in Lower Austria. *c, d:* Capital and base of a window column in the Benedictine monastery at Lorch, Württemberg. *e–g:* Two consoles and a column capital from the monastery church at Heilsbronn, Middle Franconia. *h–n:* Pillar capitals and bases in the princely crypt in the Holy Cross seminary near Vienna.

26. The seat of Count Eberhard the Elder of Württemberg in St. Amendus', Urach; carved, partially gilded oak, 1472. (Plates 27–32 show details.)

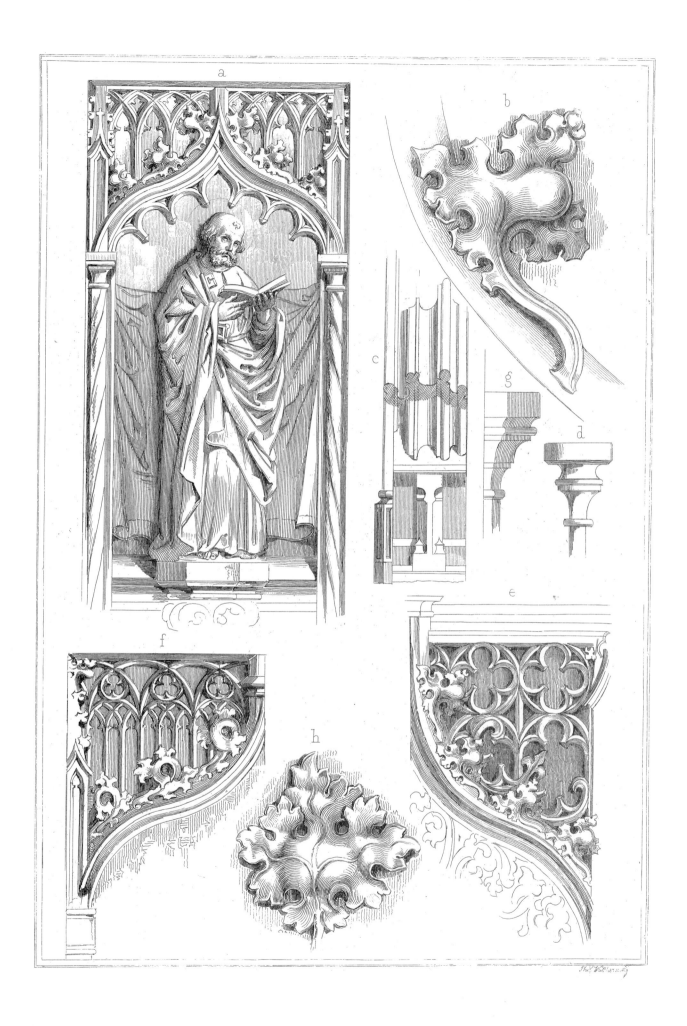

27. Detail of the seat in Plate 26.

28. Detail of the seat in Plate 26.

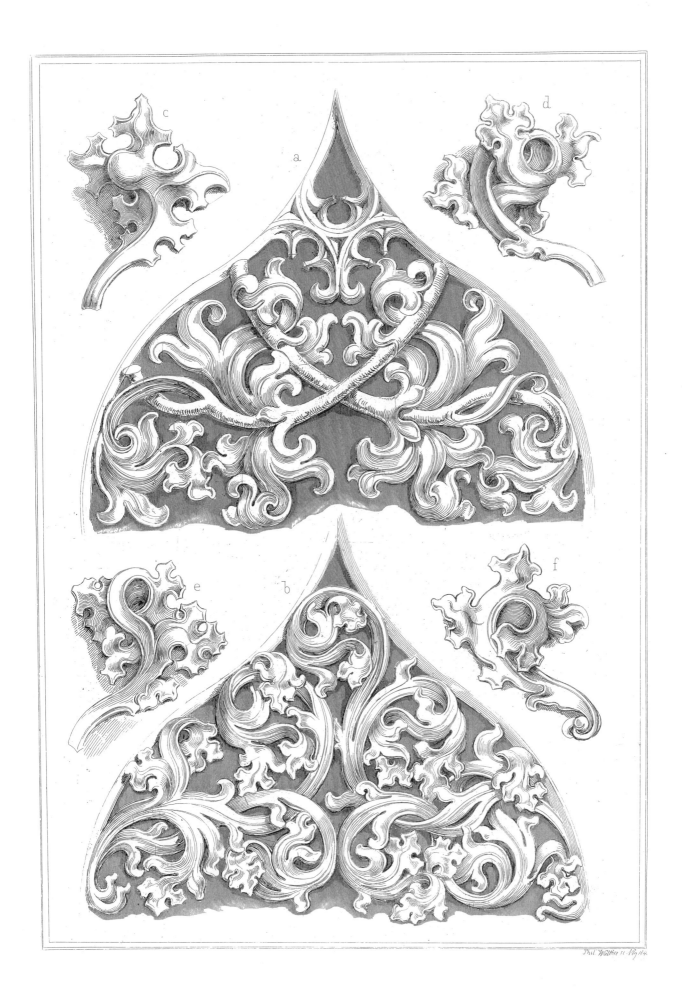

29. Detail of the seat in Plate 26.

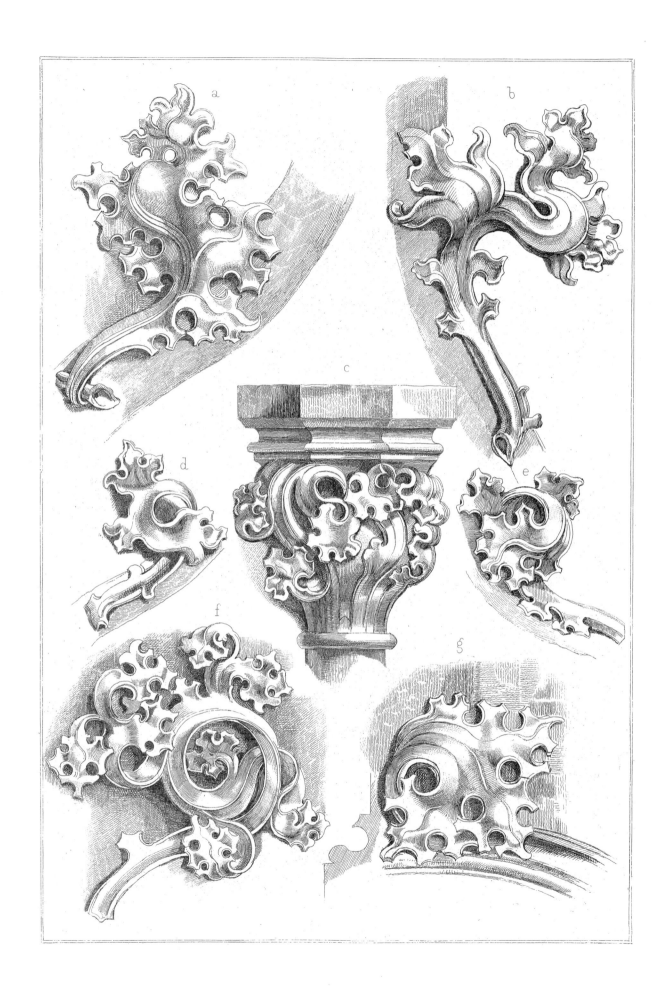

30. Detail of the seat in Plate 26.

31. Detail of the seat in Plate 26.

32. Detail of the seat in Plate 26.

33. Four column capitals and bases in the St. Walderich Chapel of the former Benedictine monastery at Murrhard.

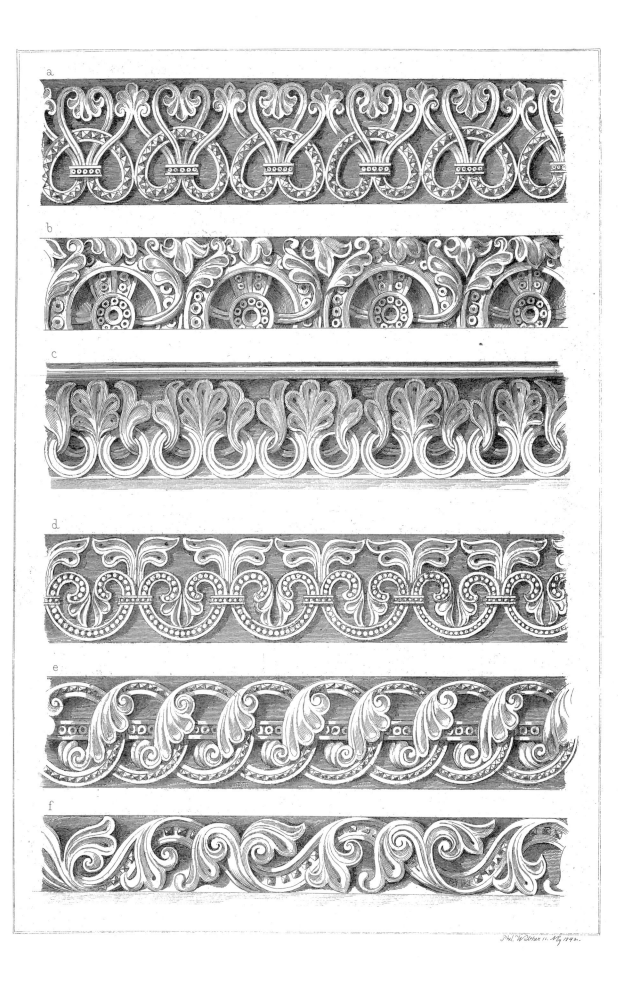

a

b

c

d

e

f

Phil. Walther u. May 1842.

34. Friezes. *a–c:* From the interior of the St. Walderich Chapel (see Plate 33). *d:* From the choir of the church at Faurndau, Göppingen, Württemberg. *e:* From a chapel in the monastery church at Alpirsbach in the Black Forest. *f:* From the former monastery at Anhausen on the Brenz.

35. Romanesque ornaments. *a–c:* Carved; from the portal of the St. Walderich Chapel, Murrhard. *d:* Painted; from the demolished chapel of the old ancestral castle of Württemberg, near Stuttgart; the numbers refer to colors (1, dark green; 2, blue-green; 3, brick red; 4, yellow; 5, green). *e:* Capital from Bamberg Cathedral. *f, g:* Vault rosettes from Bamberg Cathedral.

36. Full view *(a)* and plan *(b)* of the great column in the vestibule of the cathedral in Schwäbisch Hall. *c:* Profile of the foot of the column.

37. *a:* Sandstone capital of the grouped black schist columns in the upper chapel of the so-called New Castle at Freiburg a. d. Unstrut, near Naumburg; ornament partially gilded. *b, c, d:* Capitals and armorial eagle from the west portal of St. John's in Schwäbisch Gmünd.

38. *a:* Sandstone tympanum of a portal in the churchyard chapel, Merseburg. *b:* Column capital from Notre-Dame, Paris.

39. *a–c:* Full view, plan and profile of a tile forming the pinnacle of a green-glazed tile stove from the Dominican monastery in Nuremberg. *d:* Crocket from St. Rémy's, Rheims. *e:* Crocket from St. Kilian's, Heilbronn on the Neckar.

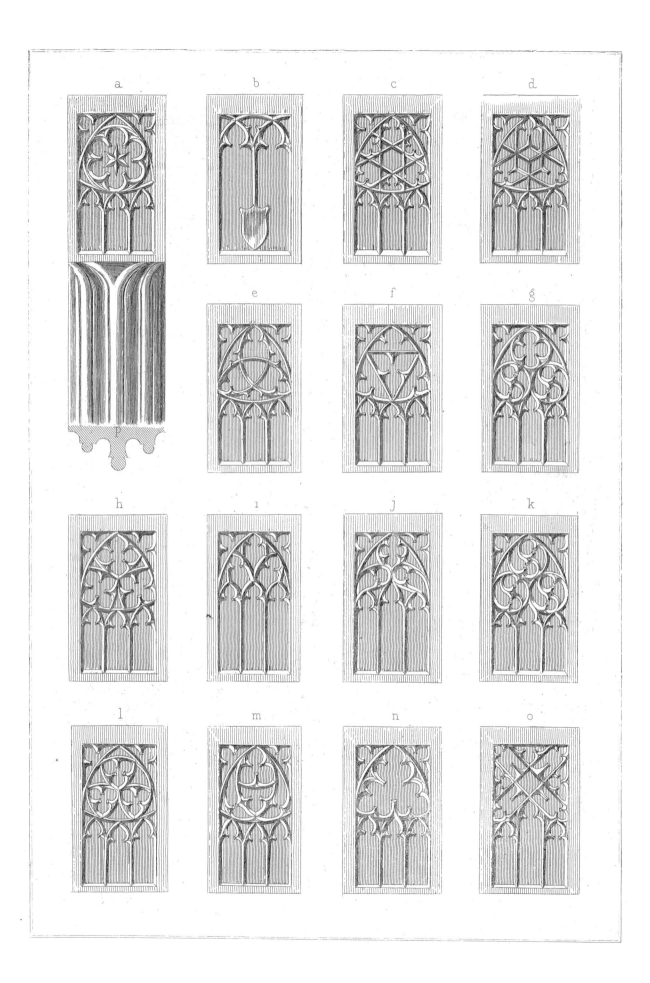

40. Carved and painted wooden ornaments on the beam ends in the summer refectory of the old parsonage of St. Lawrence's, Nuremberg.

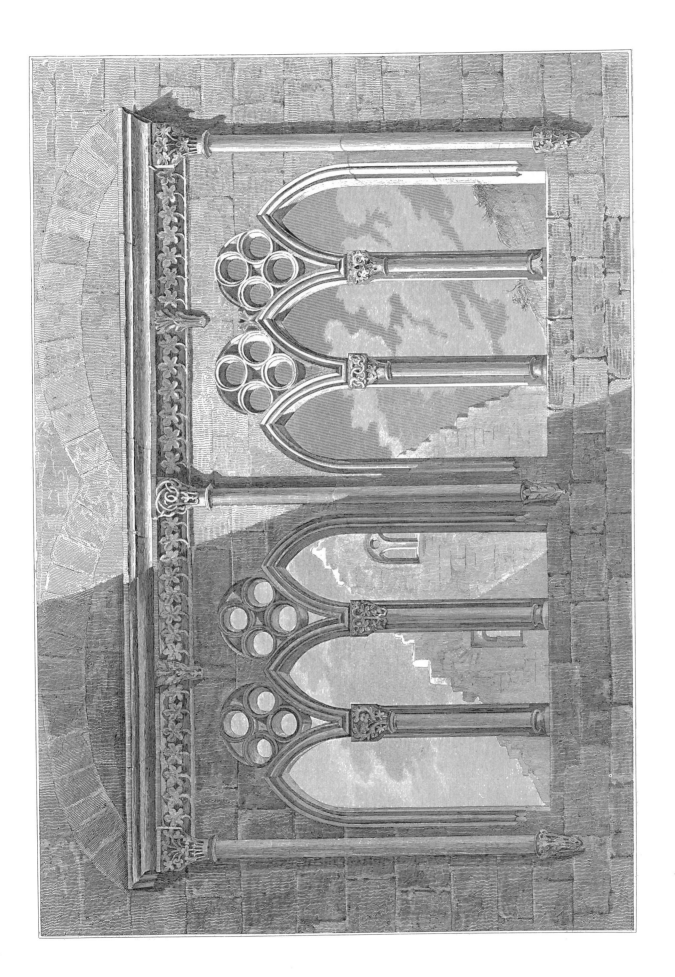

41. Windowed wall in the Saalburg, above Neustadt on the Fränkische Saale.

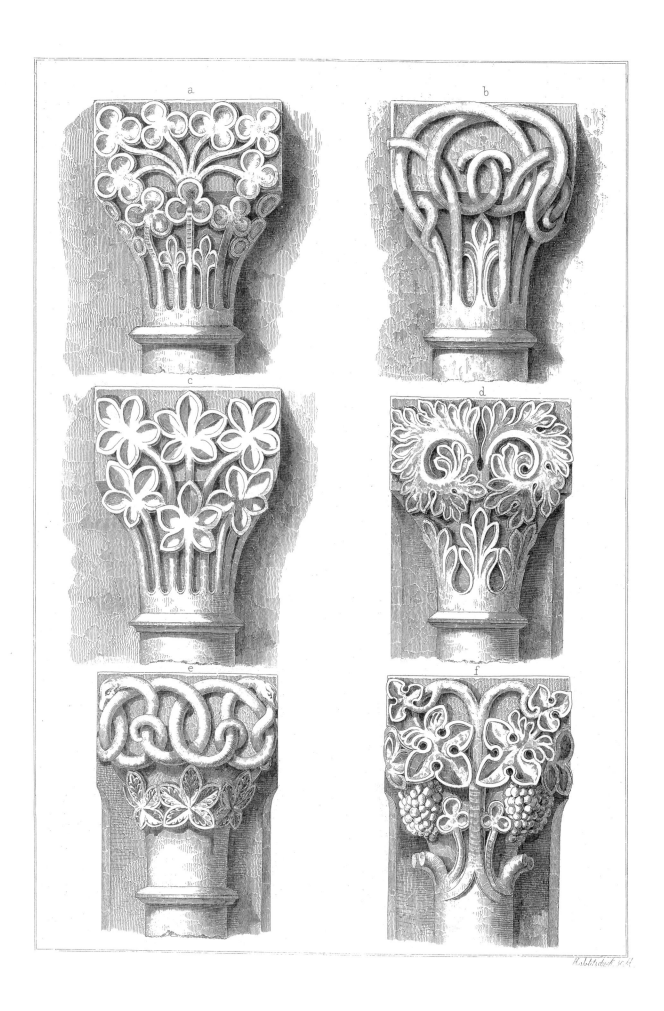

42. Larger view of the capitals shown in Plate 41.

14 F 88

Walther sc.

43. From an anonymous drawing on parchment, bearing the date 1488, of an early stage in the design of Peter Vischer's funerary monument for St. Sebald in St. Sebald's, Nuremberg (bronze monument executed 1508–1519).

44. *a:* Late Gothic capital, partially gilded, from the ruin of Hohen-Urach, Württemberg. *b, c:* Romanesque ornaments from the Württemberg ancestral castle. *d:* Late Gothic frieze, 1480, in the passage from St. Nicholas' Chapel into the collegiate church in Aachen.

45. *a:* Restored view of the relief over the door of the so-called Chapel Tower of the parish church in Rottweil, Württemberg. *b:* A frieze from the same tower.

d. Carl Mayer's Kunst-Anstalt.

46. Late Gothic ornaments. *a:* From a low-relief and openwork carved-wood Mass lectern at the high altar of the parish church at Pappenheim, with the arms of the Counts of Pappenheim. *b:* From a small maplewood casket.

47. Portal of St. Catherine's hospital church in Esslingen, built by Mathäus von Böblingen in 1470, destroyed in 1815.

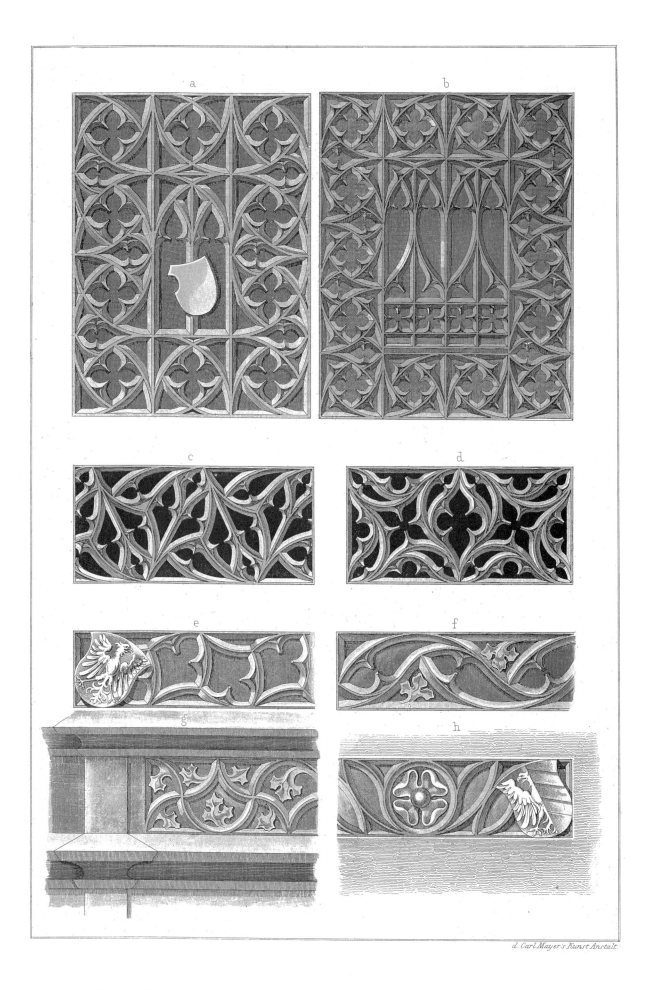

48. Late Gothic ornaments. *a:* From an oak lectern in the church of the Benedictine monastery in Blaubeuren. *b:* From a lectern in Ulm Cathedral. *c, d:* Panels from the stone gallery in the choir of the monastery church in Blaubeuren. *e–h:* Carved-wood elements from a window sill in the older part of the Nuremberg town hall.

49. *a–d:* Romanesque column capitals from the oldest part of St. Sebald's, Nuremberg.
e, f: Profiles of elements of the above capitals. *g–i:* Consoles beneath the half-columns in the same church.

50. *a, b, e, f:* Romanesque friezes of arches and consoles in the lateral nave of St. Sebald's, Nuremberg. *c, d:* Other consoles of the first frieze. *g:* Console beneath a half-column in the same church.

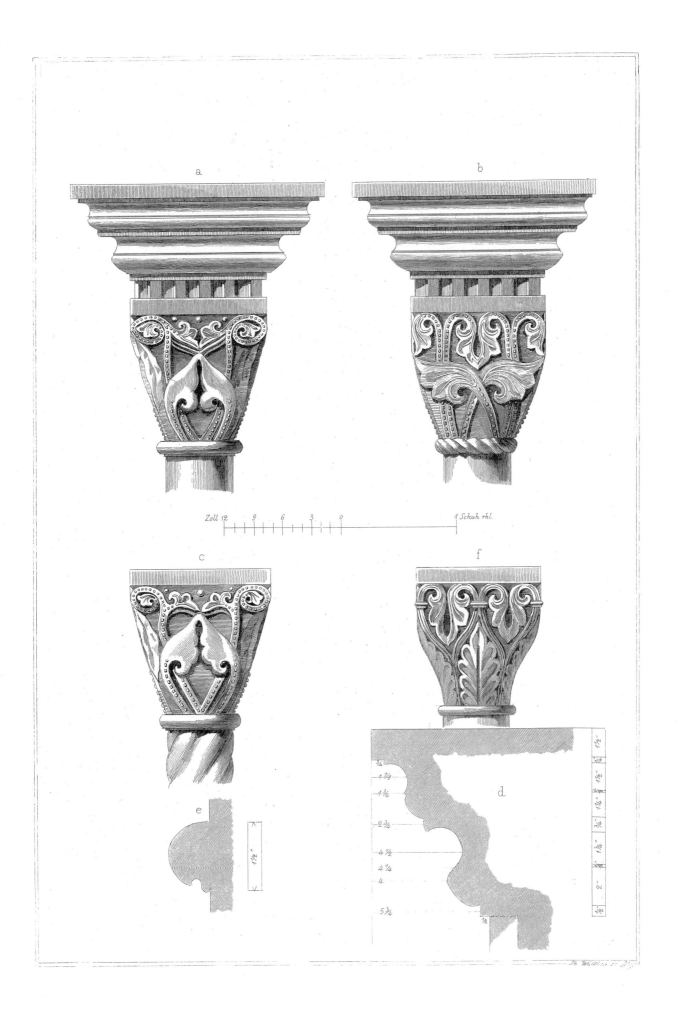

51. Four column capitals from the Burgraves' Chapel in the monastery at Heilsbronn, Bavaria, burial site of the burgraves of Nuremberg of the house of Hohenzollern. (Measurements in *Zoll* and *Schuh*, similar to inches and feet.)

Walther Sc.N59 1843

52. *a, b:* Romanesque capital from the Augustine monastery in Esslingen. *c, g, h:* Romanesque capital from the monastery church in Heilsbronn. *d, e:* Column shafts from the portal of the Burgraves' Chapel in the same monastery. *f:* Ornament on the principal cornice of the same monastery church. *i:* Window ornament from the same church.

53. Upper part of the "Schauhaus," Nuremberg, built 1522, demolished 1811. Painted stone statues of the Emperor, the seven Electors and the planets; copper guardian-statues beside the belfry.

54. Late Gothic door with the arms of Duke Ulrich of Württemberg and his wife.

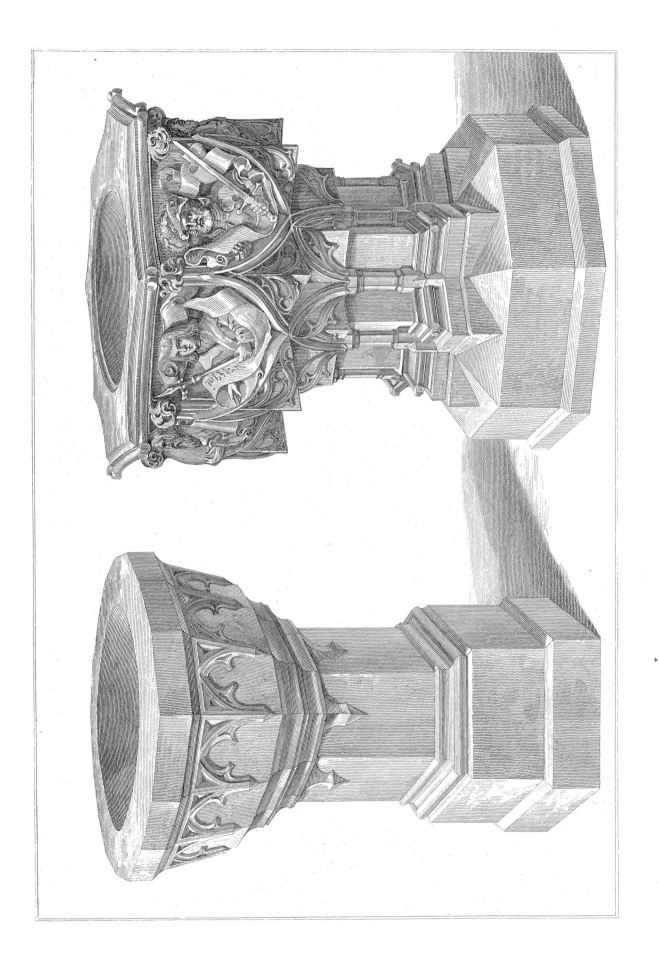

55. Baptismal fonts. *a:* From St. George's at Krafftshof, an estate of the Kress family near Nuremberg. *b:* From the parish church of St. Amendus in Urach; font dated 1518; depictions of Old Testament patriarchs, prophets and kings.

56. Tile stove in the meeting room of the parish house of St. Lawrence's, Nuremberg, which Heideloff rebuilt; the stove was newly designed by Heideloff on the basis of antique elements.

57. *a:* Grave monument of Count Ludwig of Thuringia (died 1123) in the former Benedictine monastery at Reinhardsbrunn in Thuringia. *b–g:* Romanesque ornaments. *b:* From the ruins of the monastery at Adelberg. *c:* From the monastery at Reinhardsbrunn. *d:* From the ruins of the monastery at Vesra. *e:* From the monastery at Hirschau in Württemberg. *f, g:* From the monastery at Herrenbreitungen.

58. Monument of Countess Adelheid (died 1125), wife of Count Ludwig of Thuringia, in the former monastery at Reinhardsbrunn. *b–k:* Romanesque ornaments. *b:* From the monastery at Lorch near Schwäbish Gmünd. *c:* From the monastery at Muri, Aargau, Switzerland. *d:* From the monastery at Denkendorf, Württemberg. *e:* From the monastery at Kaisersheim, near Donauwörth. *f:* From the monastery at Herrenalb, Württemberg. *g:* Console from the choir of St. John's at Crailsheim. *h:* From the choir of the monastery church at Reichenau on Lake Constance. *i:* From the monastery church at Reinhardsbrunn. *k:* Painted ornament in the former convent at Adelshausen, near Freiburg i. B.

59. Romanesque ornaments. *a*: Engraving on the sheet-metal cladding of the wooden frame of a stone portable altar; the four sacred rivers of the East, angels and cherubim. *b*: Carved ivory, from a small casket.

60. Gothic carved oak chair, possibly made in the middle of the 13th century for Count William of Holland.

61. Gothic baptismal font from the demolished pilgrimage church at Grimmenthal in Sachsen-Meiningen. The figures represent Christ on the Cross, the Virgin, the symbols of the four Evangelists and eight of the 14 "helper" saints.

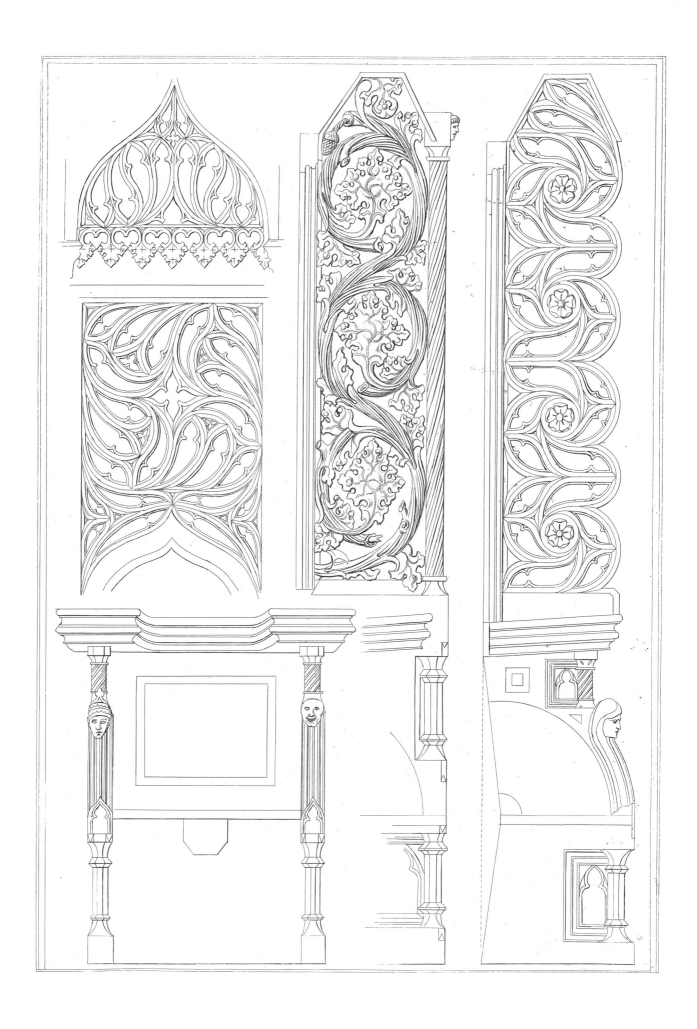

62. Details of the Late Gothic choir stalls in St. George's in the ducal palace at Altenburg an der Pleisse.

63. Details of the Late Gothic choir stalls in St. George's in the ducal palace at Altenburg an der Pleisse.

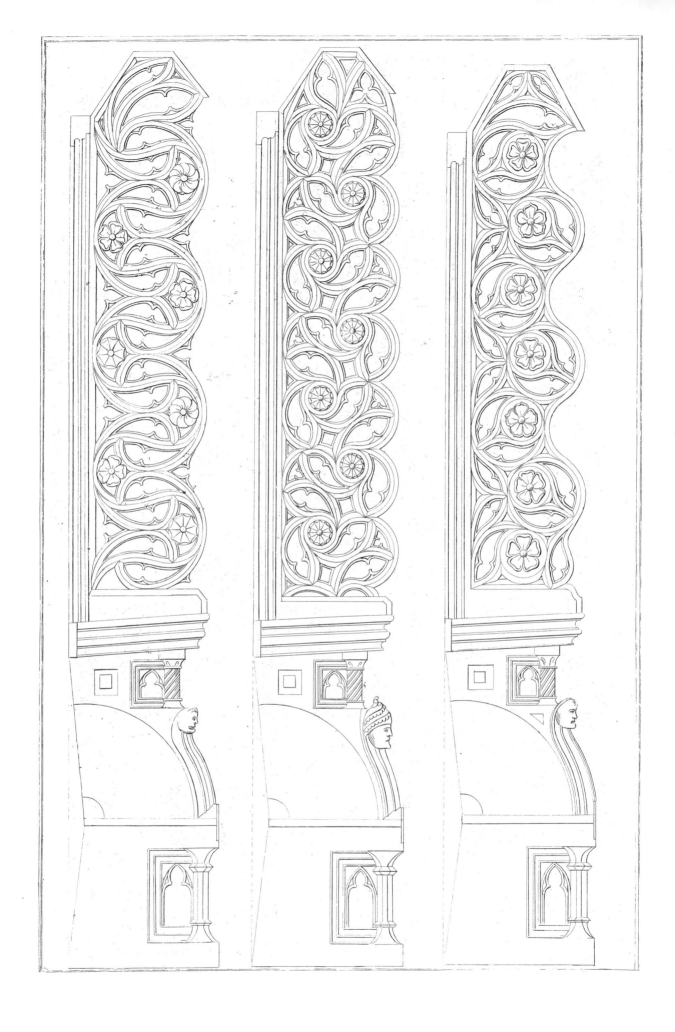

64. Details of the Late Gothic choir stalls in St. George's in the ducal palace at Altenburg an der Pleisse.

65. Romanesque ornament. *a:* Gravestone from the former cloister of the monastery at Reinhardsbrunn. *b, d:* From a painted parchment prayerbook. *c:* From the cloister of the former Benedictine monastery at Ellwangen. *e:* From the monastery at Heidenheim. *f:* From the former monastery at Herbrechtingen, Württemberg. *g:* From the monastery at Herrieden, Franconia. *h:* From the former seminary in Feuchtwangen. *i:* From the monastery at St. Gallen. *k:* From the monastery at Fulda. *l:* From the former monastery Rheinau near Konstanz. *m:* Console from the Rheims Cathedral.

66. *a:* Monument of Ludwig IV, landgrave of Thuringia (died 1172) in the monastery at Reinhardsbrunn. *b, c:* Romanesque columns on the portal of St. John's in Schwäbisch Gmünd. *d:* Capital from Notre-Dame, Paris.

67. Gothic fibula for fastening a pluvial; gilt copper with silver figures.

68. *a:* Monument of Judith, wife of Ludwig IV of Thuringia. *b, c:* Wooden columns from a courtyard gallery of a Nuremberg residence, 1516. *d:* Part of a panel in the wooden courtyard gallery of another Nuremberg house. *e:* Frieze of a Late Gothic wall cabinet in the sacristy of St. Lawrence's, Nuremberg.

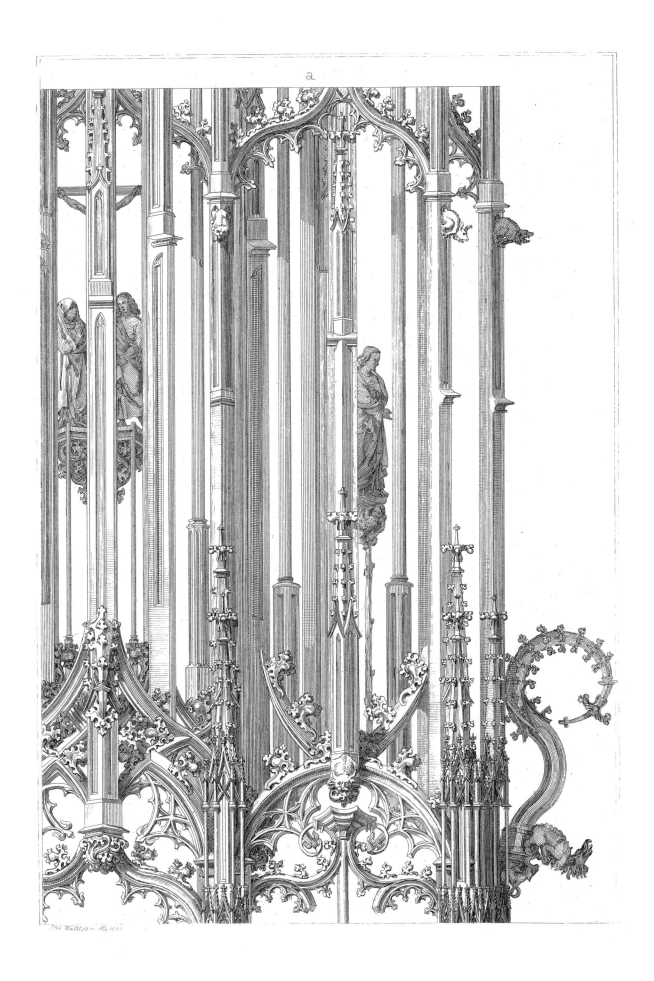

a

69. Detail of the monument described in Plate 43.

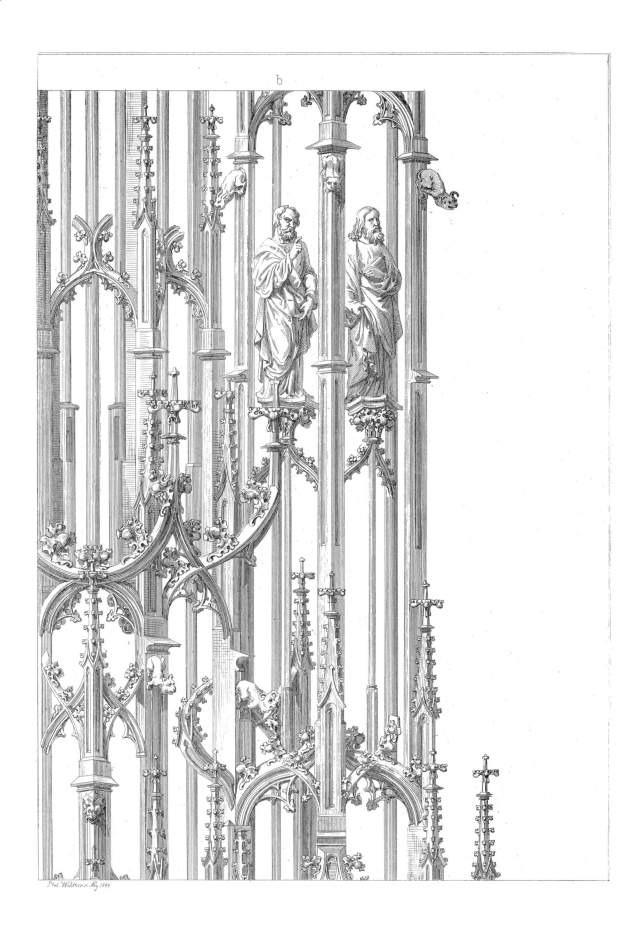

70. Detail of the monument described in Plate 43.

71. *a:* Chain of the Order of the Swan, a design by Heideloff based on an old painting, and executed in gold for the King of Prussia. *b:* Simpler chain of the same order, also based on a painting. *c:* Emblem of the Brotherhood of the Sacred Heath, with the symbol of St. Aegidius. *d:* Order of the Henneberg St. Christopher Society, founded 1490; based on the monument of the Counts of Henneberg in the collegiate Church at Schleusingen. *d:* Another sect of the same order.

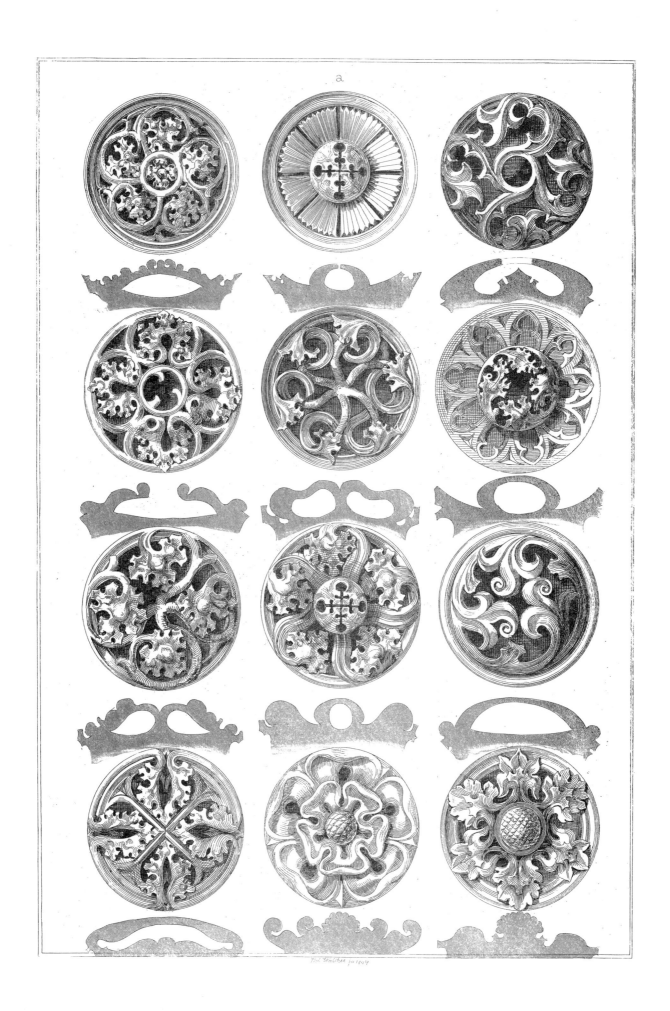

72. Rosettes from the so-called Rose Room at the princely residence on Veste Coburg.

73. Foot of a Romanesque column from St. Sebald's, Nuremberg.

74. Detail of the monument described in Plate 43.

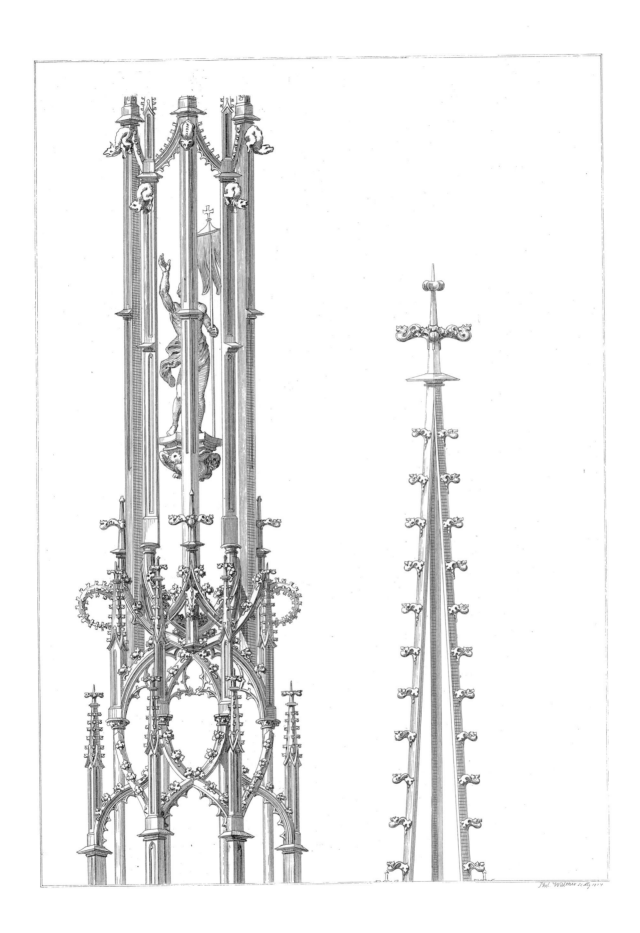

75. Detail of the monument described in Plate 43.

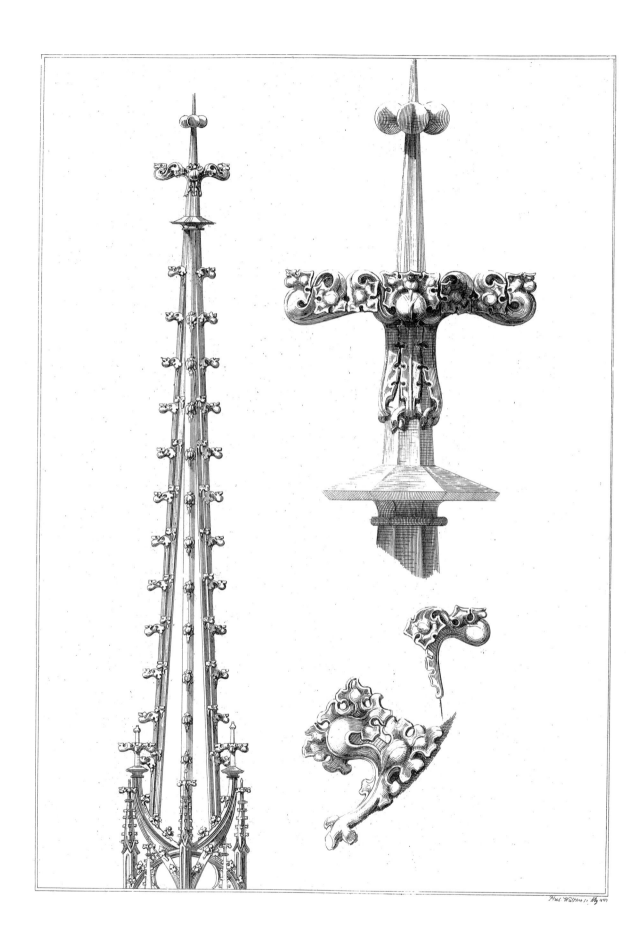

76. Detail of the monument described in Plate 43.

77. Late Gothic carved ornaments in very low relief from a residential courtyard gallery railing, Nuremberg.

78. From the same source as Plate 77.

79. From the same source as Plate 77.

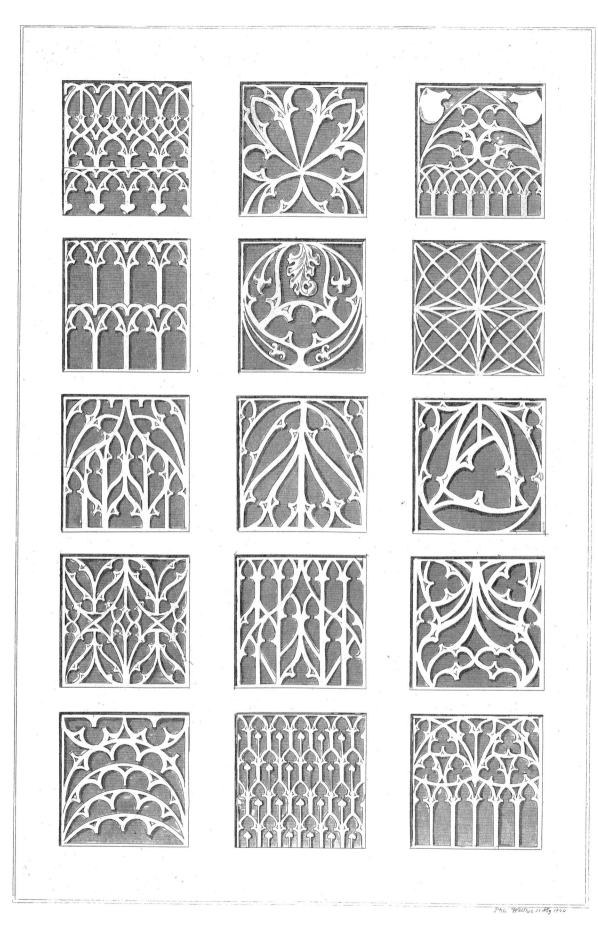

80. From the same source as Plate 77.

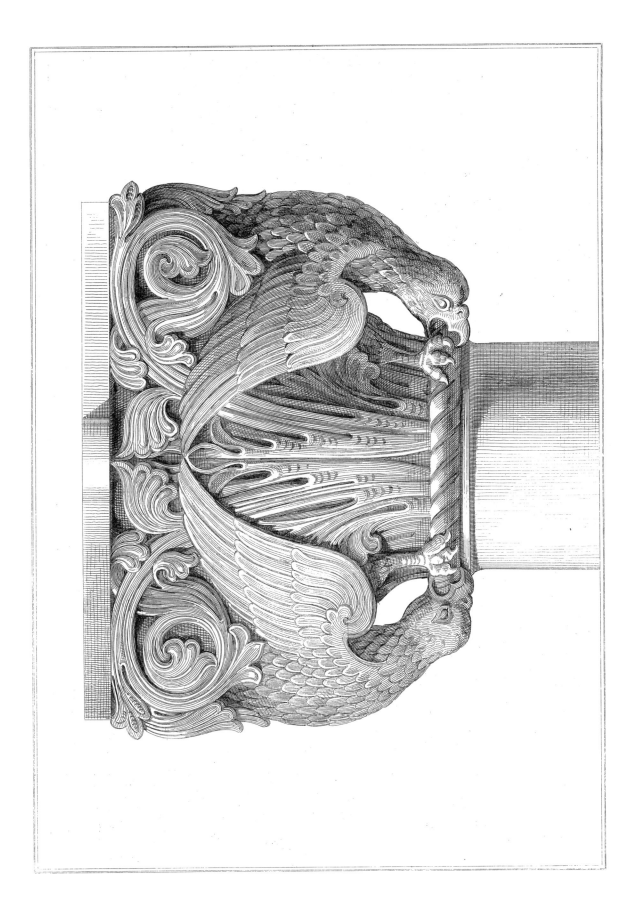

81. Romanesque column capital from the Landgraves' Room on the Wartburg, Thuringia.

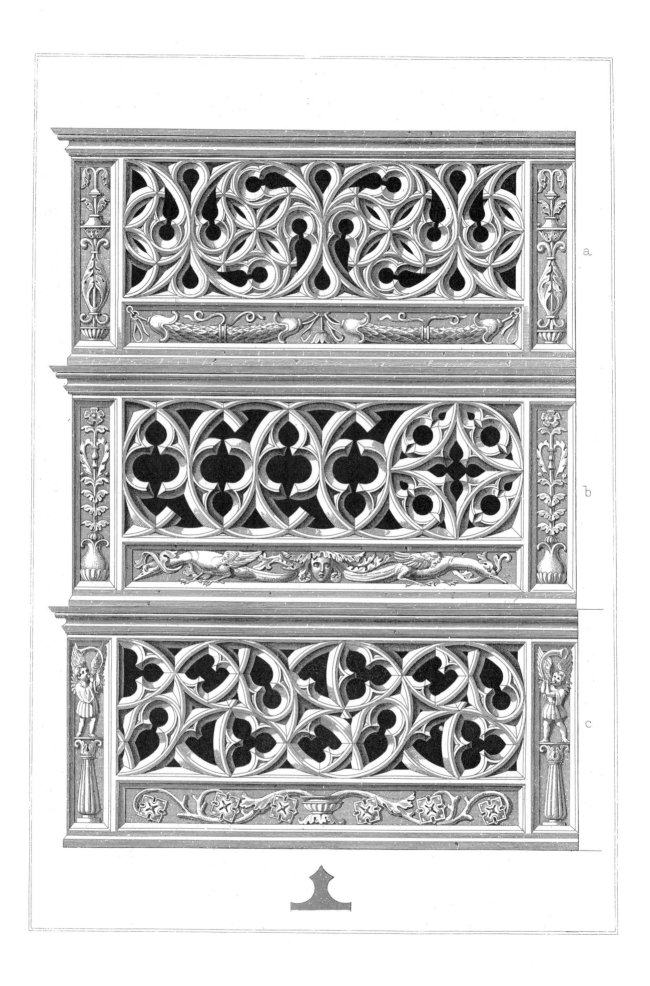

82. Elements of a wooden gallery railing from a house in Nuremberg (same house as Plate 68, *b* and *c*): main panels Late Gothic, uprights Renaissance.

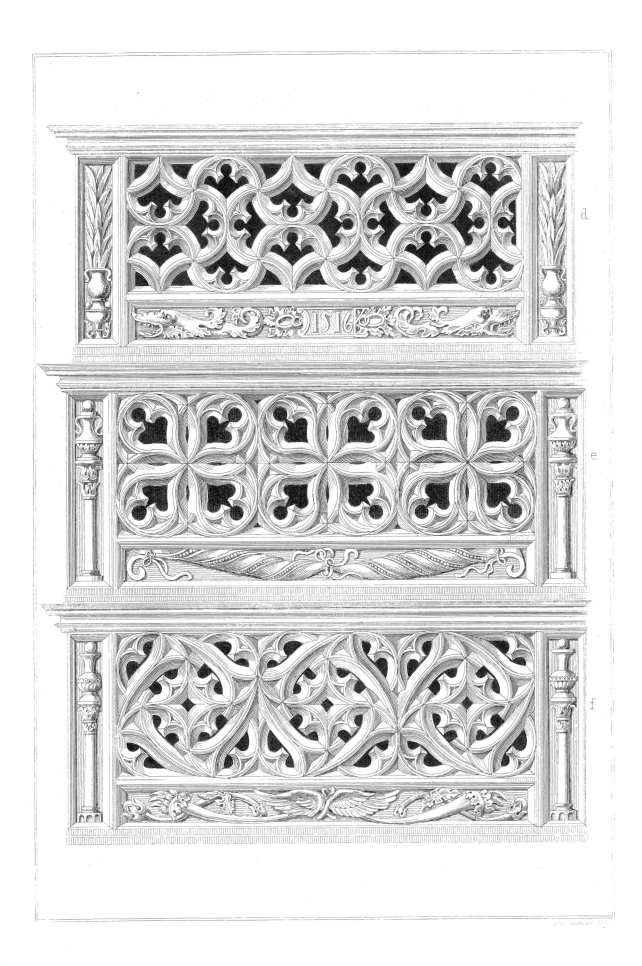

83. From the same railing as in Plate 82.

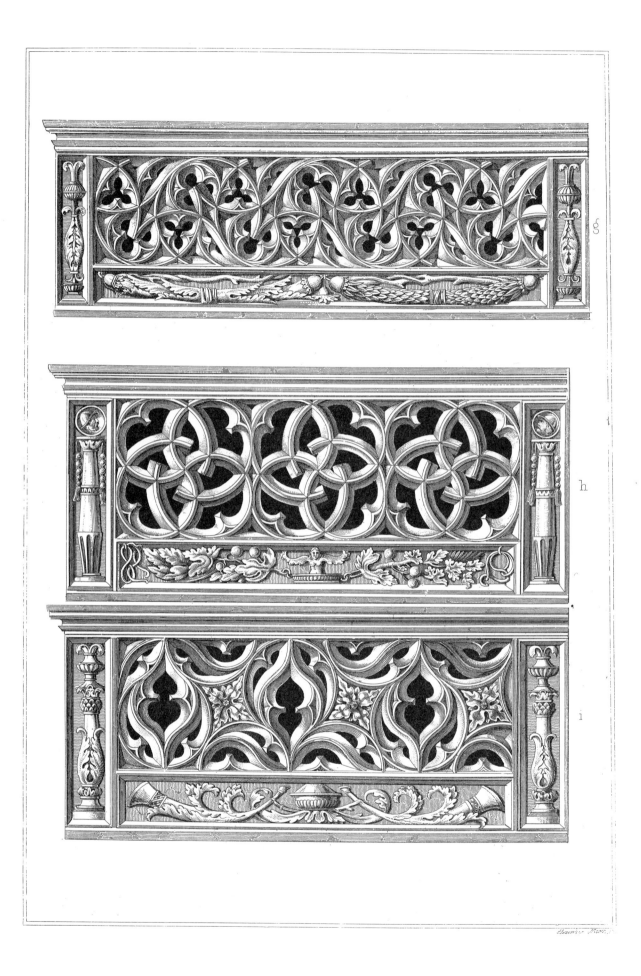

84. From the same railing as in Plate 82.

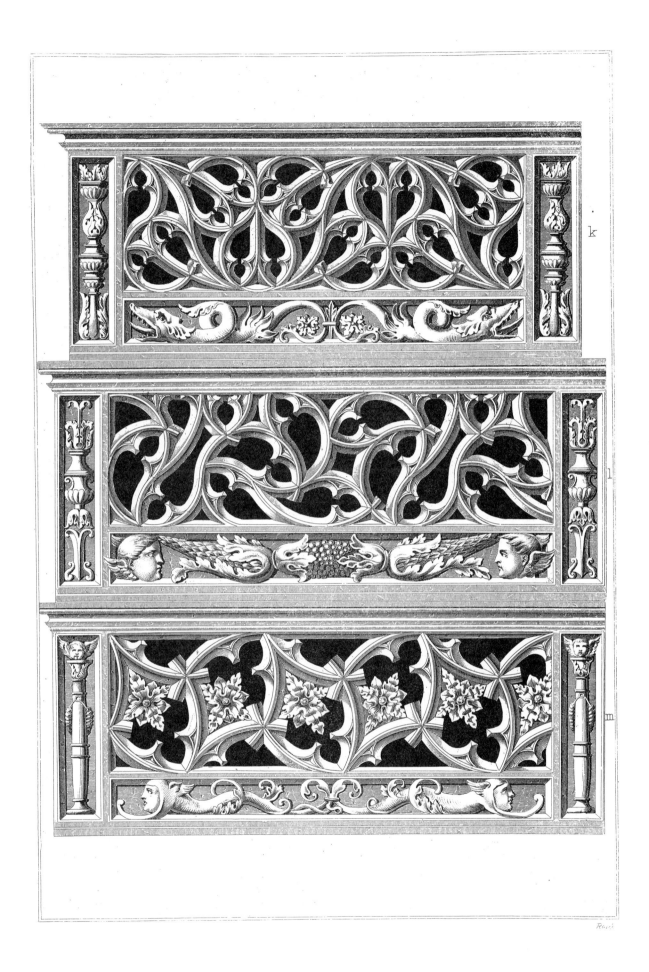

k

l

m

85. From the same railing as in Plate 82.

86. From the same railing as in Plate 77.

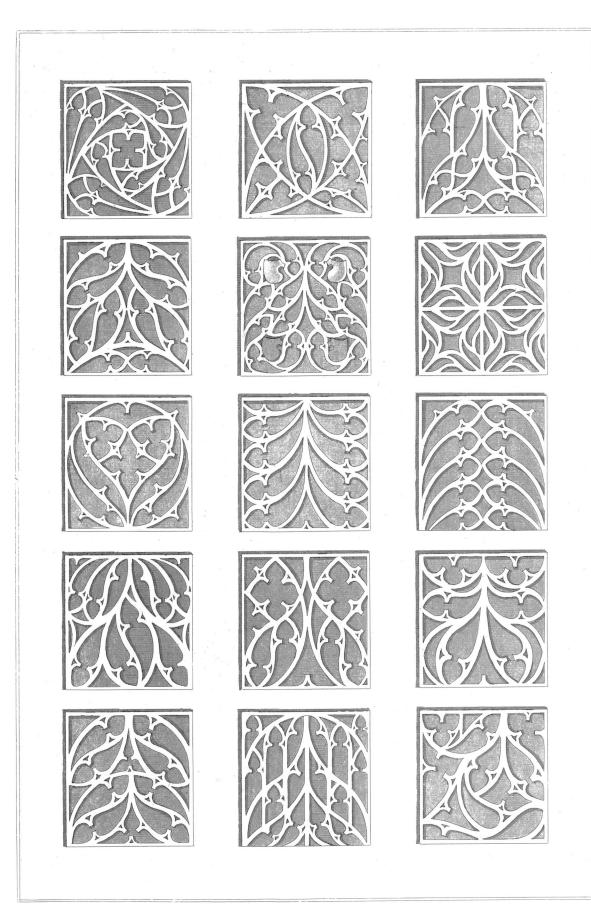

87. From the same railing as in Plate 77.

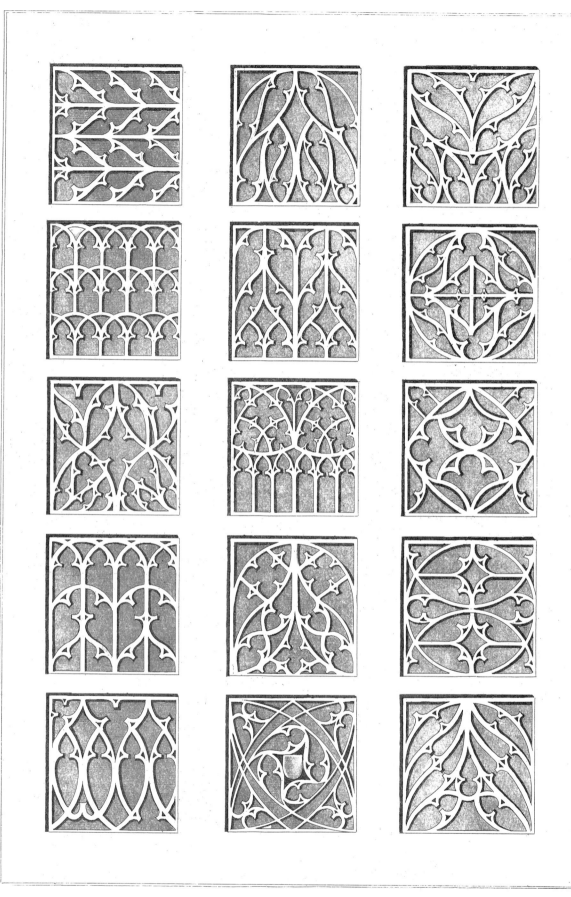

88. From the same railing as in Plate 77.

89. Romanesque ornaments. *a–c:* Column capitals from the monastery church at Faurndau near Göppingen. *d:* Column capital from the former monastery at Herbrechtingen. *e–g:* Column bases from the monasteries at Forch, Faurndau and the island of Rheinau, respectively.

Hauteur du fût de la colonne quatre fois et demi le diamètre.

Die Höhe des Stammes der Säule hat 4½ mal die Breite des Durchmessers.

Height of column shaft is four and a half times the diameter.

90. Romanesque joined columns from the Wartburg.

91. Sacrament house door in St. Sebald's, Nuremberg; wood painted red, iron trim gilded.

92. Paneling and door in the so-called Emperor's Room in the Scheurl house, Nuremberg.

93. *a–d:* Railing and date of the stone gallery in the courtyard of a Nuremberg residence, 1498. *e, f:* Late Gothic carved-wood ornaments from Hohenstein in Württemberg, once owned by Heideloff.

94. Late Gothic silver-gilt goblet of 1510.

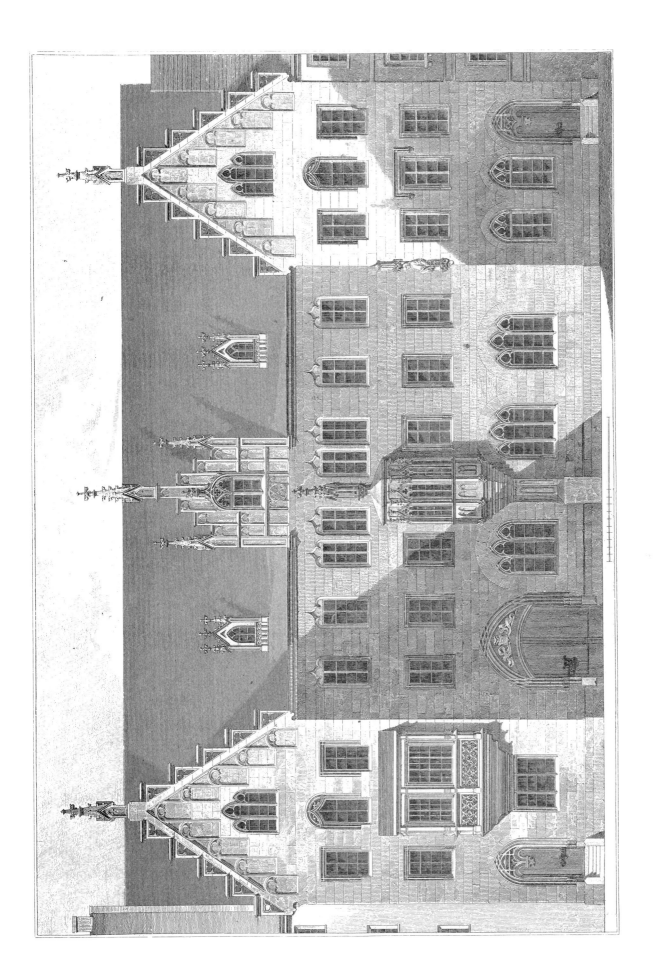

95. The new parsonage of St. Lawrence's, Nuremberg: an enlarged restoration by Heideloff, ca. 1840, incorporating late-15th-century elements.

96. *a–c:* Stone figures (wives of German rulers) from abutments of cross-vaulting in the open gallery of the 1580 "Lusthaus" in Stuttgart. *d:* Late Gothic funerary monument from the Dominican monastery in Esslingen.

Fig. a

97. Elements of a painted wooden ceiling in the Nuremberg citadel from the era of
Holy Roman Emperor Charles IV (reigned 1355–1378).

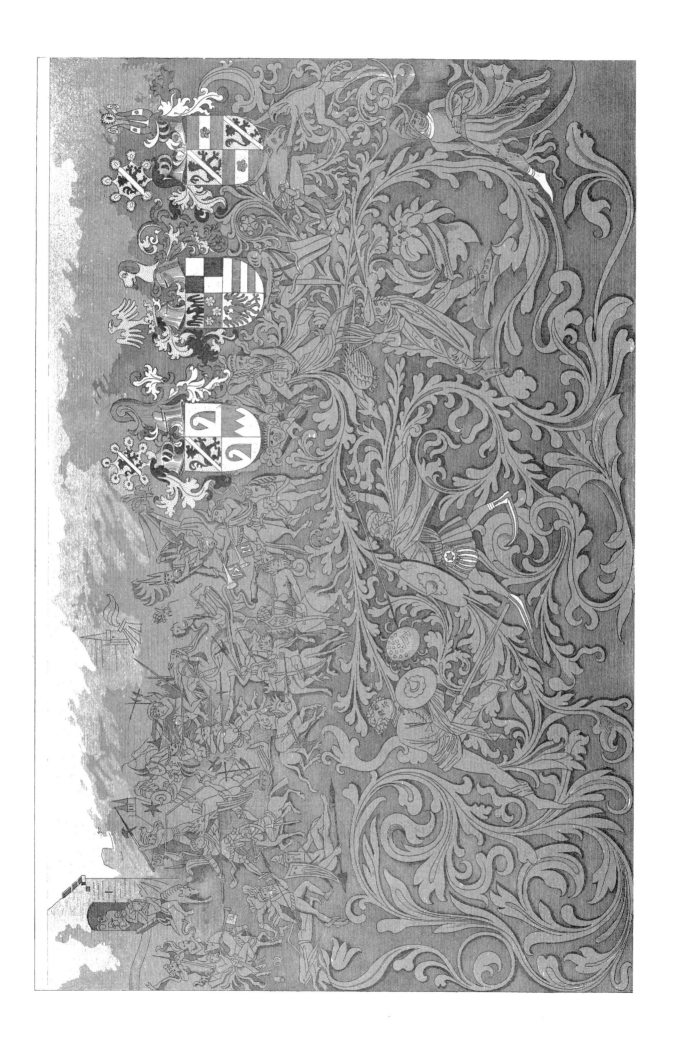

98. Wall painting in the old parsonage of St. Lawrence's, Nuremberg, possibly depicting a battle between Germans and Hussites early in the 15th century.

99. Three Gothic wooden doors from the parsonage of St. Lawrence's, Nuremberg; *c* is dated 1504.

100. Late Gothic window enframements. *a*: From the monastery at Bebenhausen, Württemberg. *b*: From the Reichenauer monastery yard in Ulm. *c*: From the old parsonage of St. Lawrence's, Nuremberg, dated 1458. *d*: From a private residence in Nördlingen.

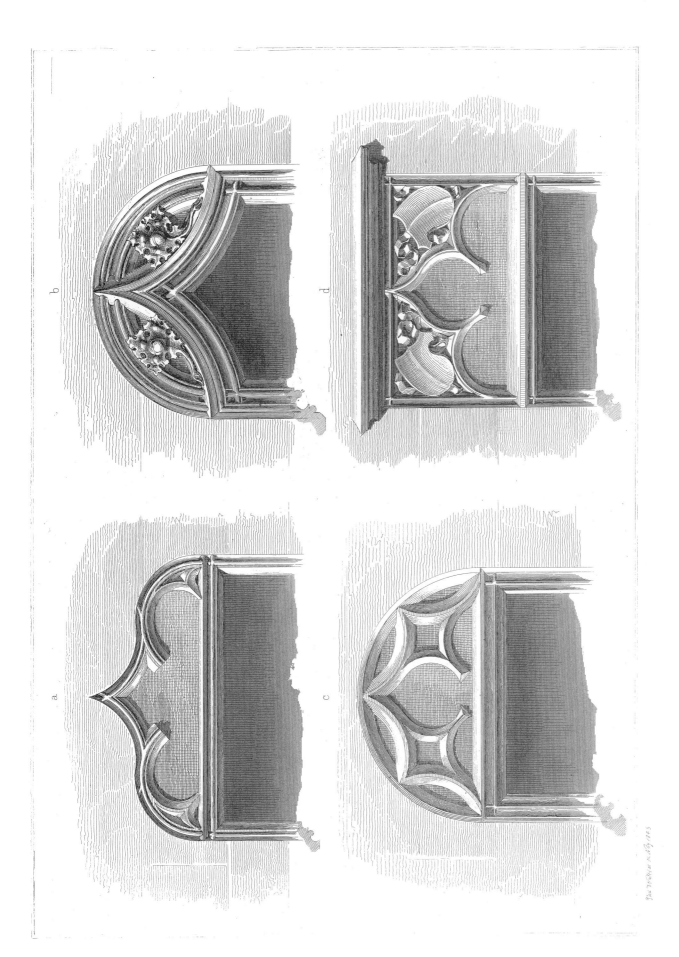

101. Late Gothic window enframements. *a*: From the Nuremberg city hall. *b*: From the gable of the Dominican monastery church, Nuremberg. *c*, *d*: From the old hospital in Esslingen.

102. Door from the Emperor's Room in the Scheurl house, Nuremberg.

103. "Bridal door" from St. Lawrence's, Nuremberg (restored by Heideloff in 1824), with figures of St. Lawrence and St. Leonhard.

104. Painting on parchment of Sebald Schreier (1446–1520), Nuremberg city councillor, referring to the donation of a chapel and altar in St. Sebald's in Schwäbisch Gmünd.

105. Romanesque ornaments in the monastery church at Alpirsbach in the Black Forest. *a:* Baptismal font. *b:* Decoration near the top of the inner surface of the font. *c:* Pillar capital.

106. *a:* Romanesque column capital from the monastery church at Alpirsbach. *b:* Head of Christ from a ruined monastery church in Mainz.

107. Romanesque ornament. *a:* Cornice of a ruined chapel in the monastery at Gengenbach, Baden. *b:* Pillar capital from St. Pelagius' in the old quarter of Rottweil, Württemberg. *c:* Column capital in the Bamberg Cathedral. *d:* Capital from the portal of the monastery at Vesra.

108. Late Gothic baptismal font (with various sections) from the old church at Oberlind near Sonneberg in Saxony.

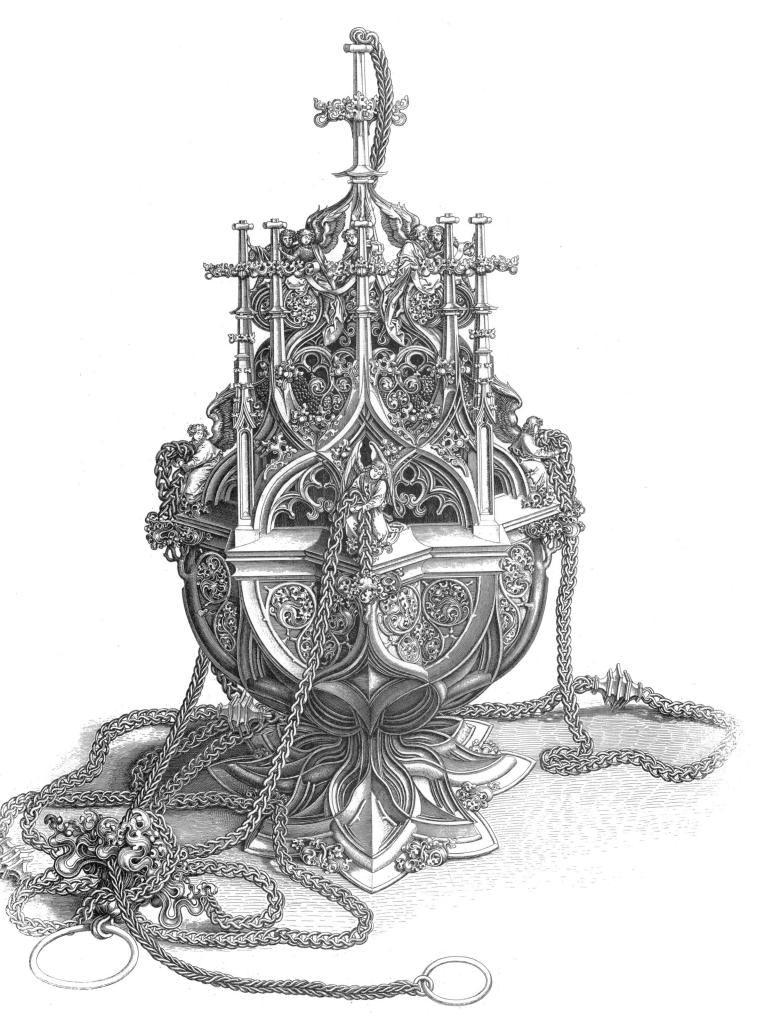

109. Late Gothic censer, from a copperplate engraving by Martin Schongauer (died 1491).

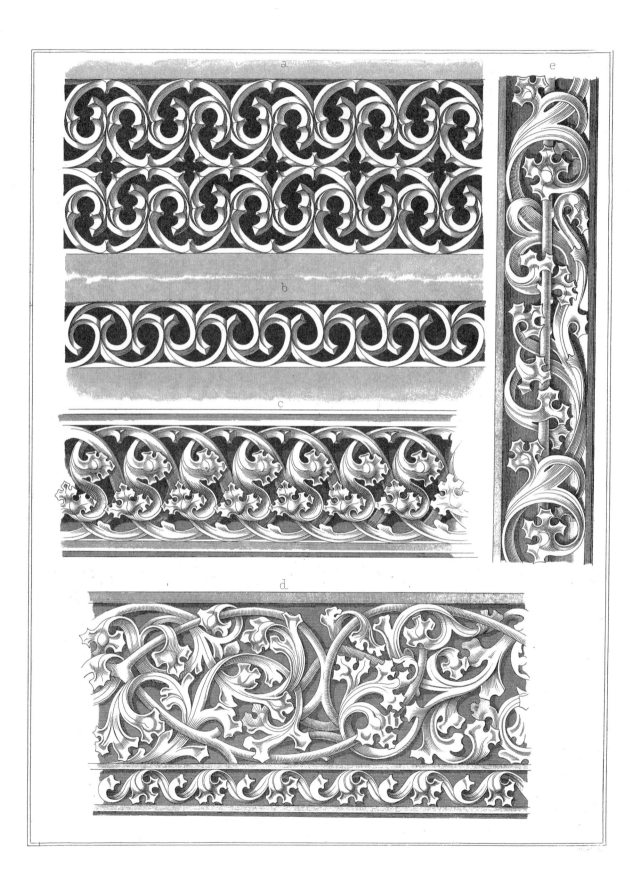

110. Late Gothic ornament. *a, b:* From an altar in the Church of the Holy Cross at Rottweil in the Black Forest. *c:* From the provost's house at Herrnburg. *d:* From a sacristy cabinet in St. Michael's, Schwäbisch Hall. *e:* From a carved oak choir stall in a church in Siedelfingen, Württemberg.

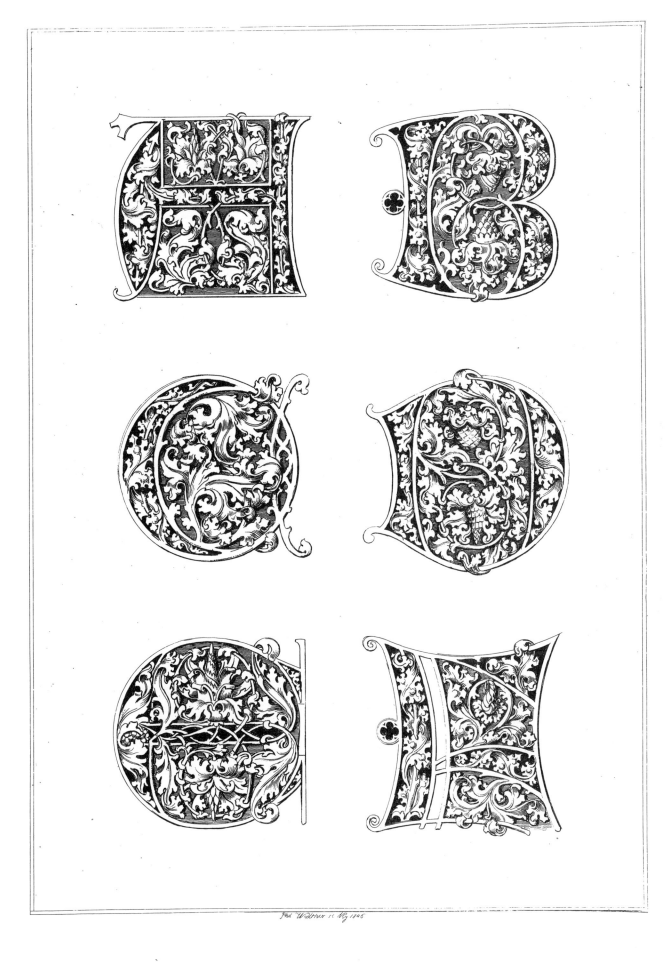

111. Late Gothic initials from various manuscripts, painted and gilded on parchment.

112. Late Gothic initials from various manuscripts, painted and gilded on parchment.

113. *a, b:* Romanesque cornices from the tower of St. John's, Schwäbisch Gmünd.
c: Romanesque cornice from the tower of St. Martin's, Feuchtwangen. *d:* Cornice from
the former town hall, Saalfeld.

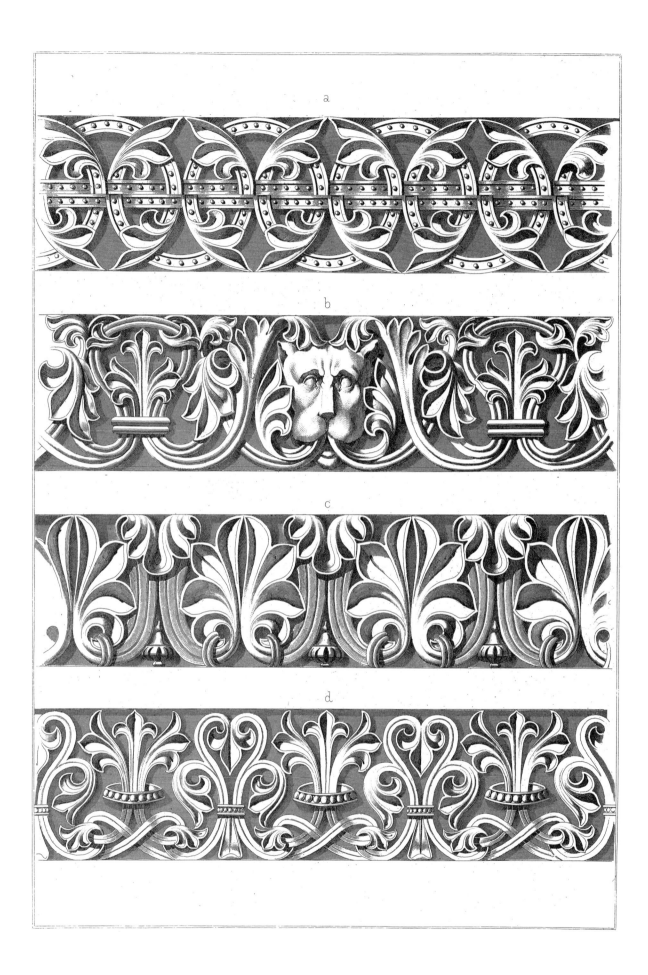

a

b

c

d

114. Romanesque friezes from the former town hall, Saalfeld.

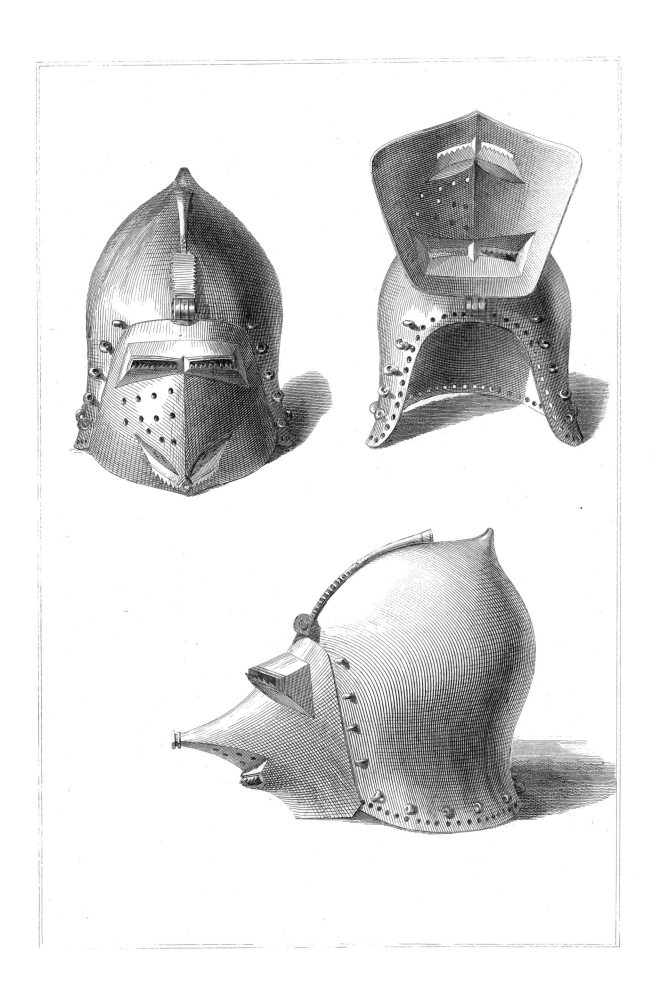

115. Helmets in the hall of armor on the Veste Coburg.

116. Gothic baptismal fonts. *a:* From the principal church in Weissenburg. *b:* From Männerstadt an der Lauer, Bavaria.

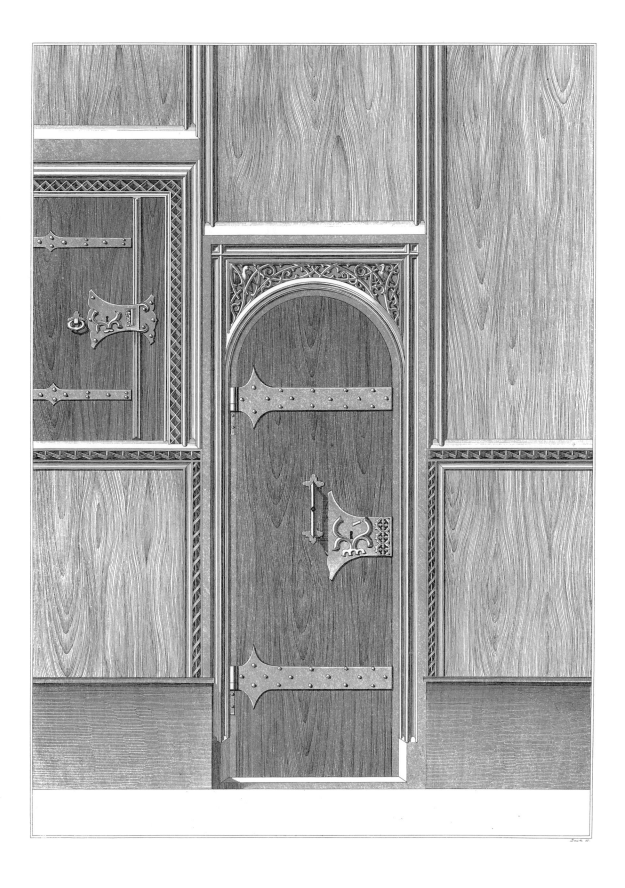

117. Door in the Emperor's Room in the Scheurl house, Nuremberg.

118. Late Gothic table with carved and inlaid decoration, allegedly dating from 1508, from the Benedictine monastery at Weissenohe, Upper Franconia.

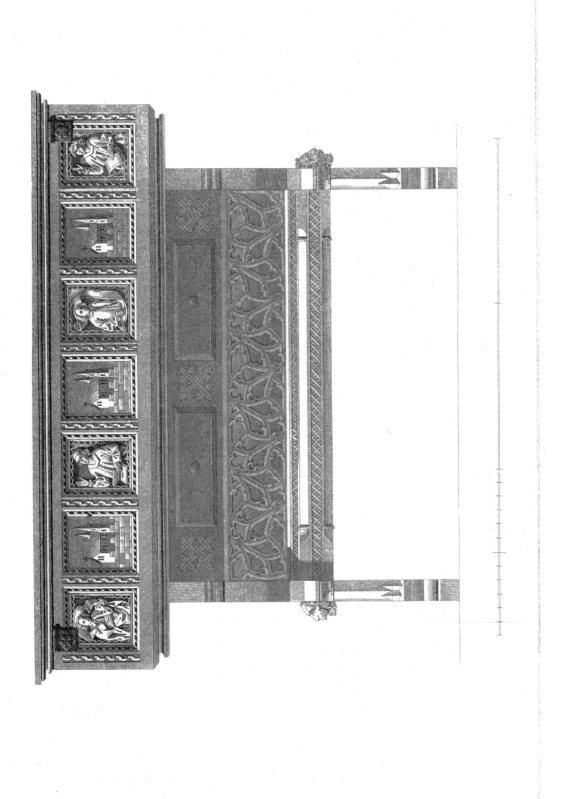

119. Another view of the table in Plate 118.

120. Baldachin over the statue of the Virgin in the altarpiece in the monastery at Blaubeuren.

121. *a:* Late Gothic pinnacle of a stone fountain in the marketplace at Rottenburg on the Neckar. *b, c:* Plan and profile of the base of the pinnacle. *d, e:* Late Gothic consoles from the Holy Sepulchre in St. Mary's, Reutlingen. *f:* Console of a crossvaulting in the chapel of the former Waldburg of the Counts of Zimmern. *g:* Wooden low-relief backrests of the choir stalls in the village church at Wilmadingen, near Lichtenstein castle.

F. Wagner sc.

122. Painted and gilded limestone relief in the collegiate church in Stuttgart, with the arms of Württemberg, Savoy, Cleve and Bavaria.

123. *a:* Late Gothic portal in the former monastery at Mönchröden near Sonneberg; the door is by Heideloff. *b:* Part of a room in the same monastery. *c:* Part of the ceiling of the same room.

124. Door from Ober-Kranichfeld.

125. Ornaments from a stone tabernacle once in the hospital church at Esslingen, built by Mathäus von Böblingen in 1470.

126. *a:* Roland column on the outside staircase of the town hall of Heilbronn on the Neckar. *b:* Design for the restoration of a similar column in Zerbst.

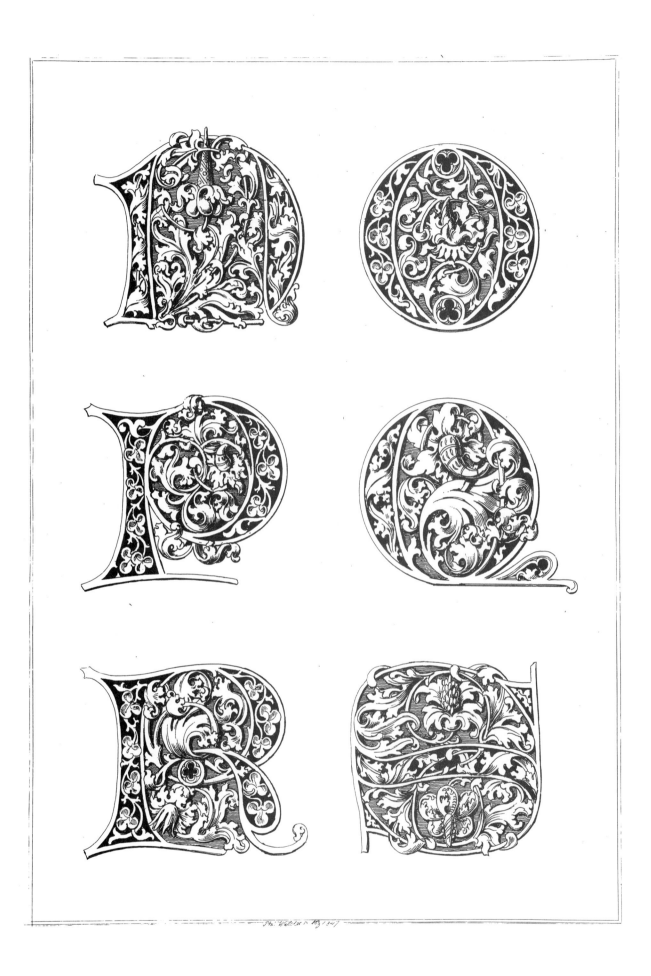

127. Initials (continuation of the alphabet on Plates 111 and 112).

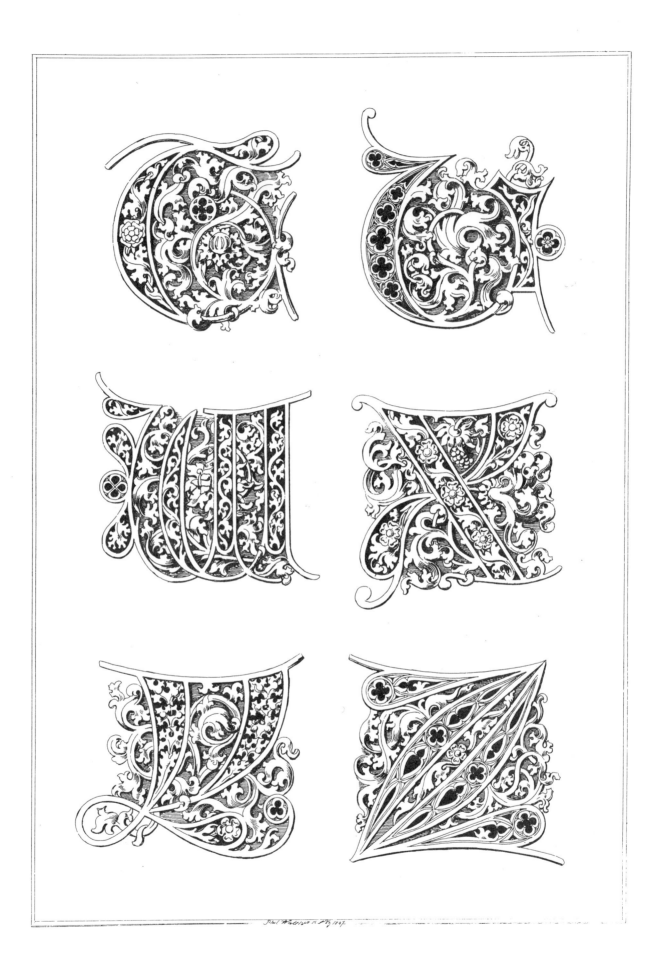

128. Initials (continued).

129. Details from the Romanesque church at Faurndau.

130. Column capital and base from the baptismal chapel of the monastery at Comburg near Schwäbisch Hall.

131. Portal of the former St. Nicholas Chapel on St. Lawrence's Square, Nuremberg.

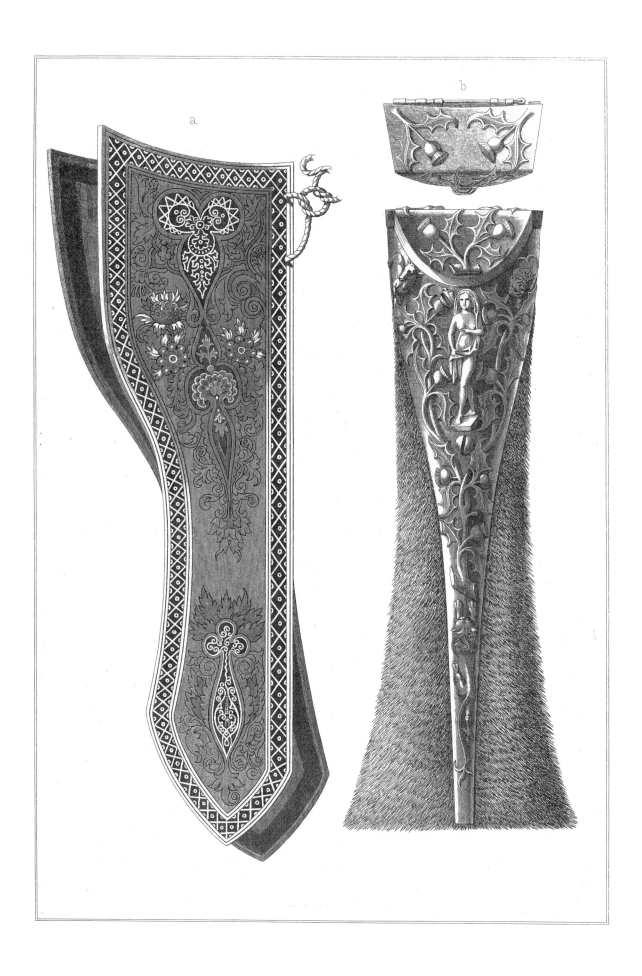

132. *a:* Bow cover from a painting by Dürer in the Nuremberg citadel. *b:* Wooden quiver trimmed with badger fur; iron cover; from a Berlin collection.

133. Bay window/balcony known as the "Golden Roof" from a house in the market square, Innsbruck; the background and fountain are Heideloff's invention.

A. Marx sc

134. Late Gothic chair from the old armory in Nuremberg, possibly as restored in Heideloff's imagination.

135. Late Gothic oak door from the dormitory of the former monastery at Denkendorf.

136. Unexecuted design by Heideloff for the base of a statue of Dürer in Nuremberg, with figures and medallions of Dürer's chief pupils.

137. Romanesque ornament from the monastery church at Heilsbronn, Bavaria. *a–c:*
Column capital and base. *d–f:* Feet of columns. *g:* Low-relief decoration.

138. *a:* Frieze with consoles from an Arabic-style palace in Palermo. *b, c:* Romanesque capitals from Knautheim. *d:* Romanesque capital from the citadel chapel at Hohenlohe, Saxony. *e, 1:* Capital and base in the upper room of the double chapel in Hohenlandsberg Castle near Leipzig. *f, 2:* Romanesque capital and base in St. Bernard's, Frankfurt am Main. *g, 3:* Romanesque capital and base in the old castle at Cobern on the Moselle.

139. *a:* Gravestone with the arms of Württemberg in the church at Beutelsbach. *b–e:* Crosses (*b*, stone, from a gable of the monastery at Frauenrotha; *c*, from a gable of the church at Mellrichstadt; *d*, from the tower of the church at Brennet; *e*, from the gable of the church in Beutelsbach). *f, g:* Heads from the church at Brennet. *h:* Window from the same church. *i:* Head from the church at Beutelsbach. *k, l:* Capital from the Nuremberg citadel.

140. "Bridal door," late 14th century, of St. Sebald's, Nuremberg, with planned restorations by Heideloff; statues of the wise and foolish virgins.

141. Late Gothic crosier, from a copperplate engraving by Martin Schongauer (died 1491).

Alex. Maes del. Aug.

142. The Nuremberg city hall as it was in 1580.

143. Courtyard of the new Nuremberg city hall with vestiges of the old (early 16th-century) town hall.

144. Columns resting on corbels below the gallery depicted on Plate 143.

145. *a:* Center of an embroidered antependium in the church at Komburg near Schwäbisch Hall. *b:* Repoussé silver head of Christ on a velvet background, probably from an antependium. *c, d:* Romanesque copper-gilt candlesticks with enamel decoration. *e:* Romanesque Communion cup. *f, g:* Painted festival crosses (*f,* from the monastery church at Weiler near Esslingen; *g,* from the church of St. Catherine's convent, Nuremberg).

146. Gothic bronze water fountain for a hand-washing basin. The taps are Heideloff's invention.

147. Pinnacle of a Late Gothic silver-gilt monstrance from the old monastery at Rottweil.

148. Late Gothic copper-gilt monstrance in the Catholic church in Coburg.

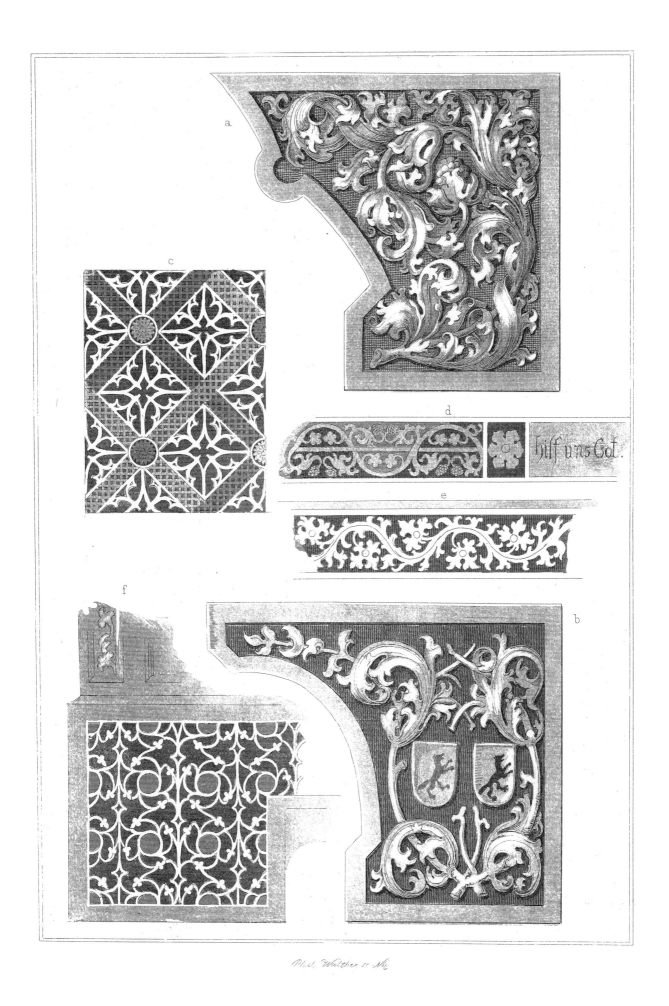

149. *a, b:* Consoles of the wings of a Late Gothic altarpiece. *c:* Silk fabric used as an antependium. *d:* Silk border. *e:* Cloth border. *f:* Foot of a Gothic oak church cabinet with inlays.

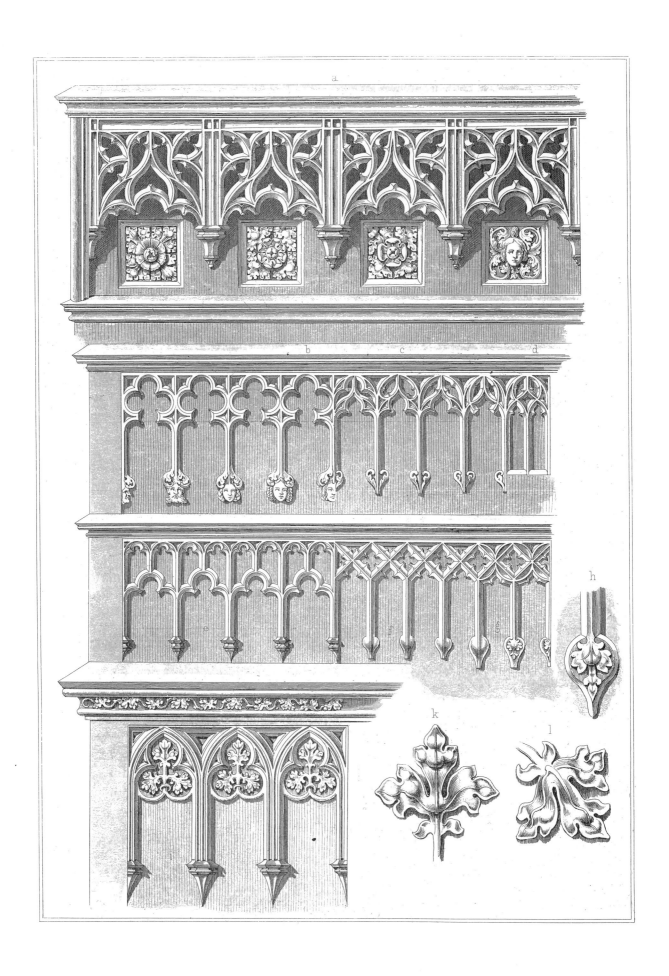

150. Late Gothic cornice decoration. *a:* From the Archbishop's palace in Palermo. *b, e,
i, k, l:* From the parish church at Bamberg. *c:* From a monastery building at Blaubeuren.
d, f: From the monastery at Adelberg in Württemberg.

151. Cresting of a tabernacle in the Halberstadt Cathedral.

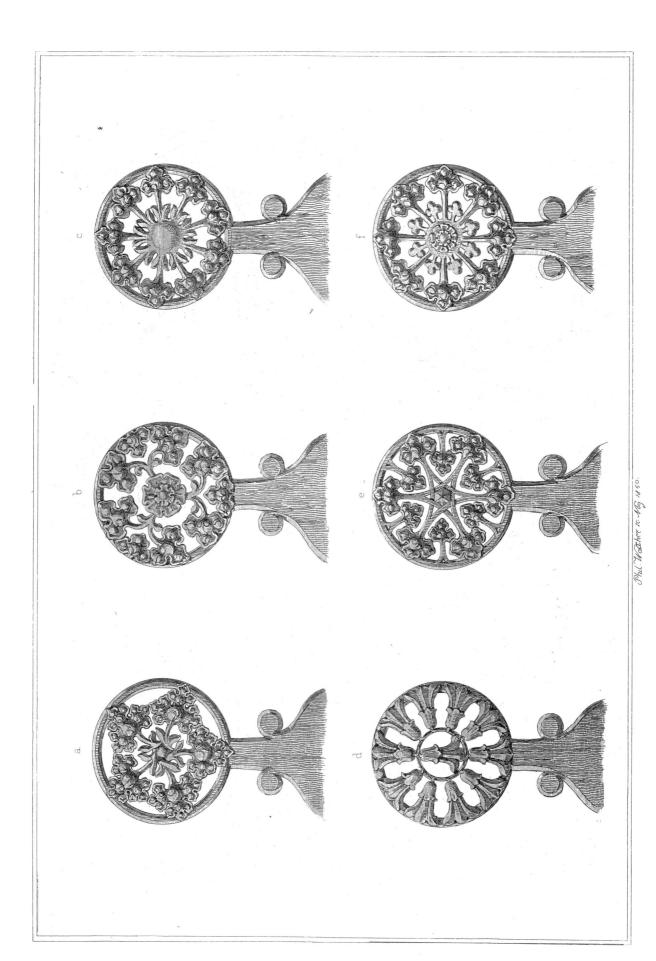

Phil. Walther sc. July 1850.

152. Ornaments from the choir stalls in the Halberstadt Cathedral.

153. Romanesque baptismal font from St. Michael's, Altenstadt, Upper Bavaria.

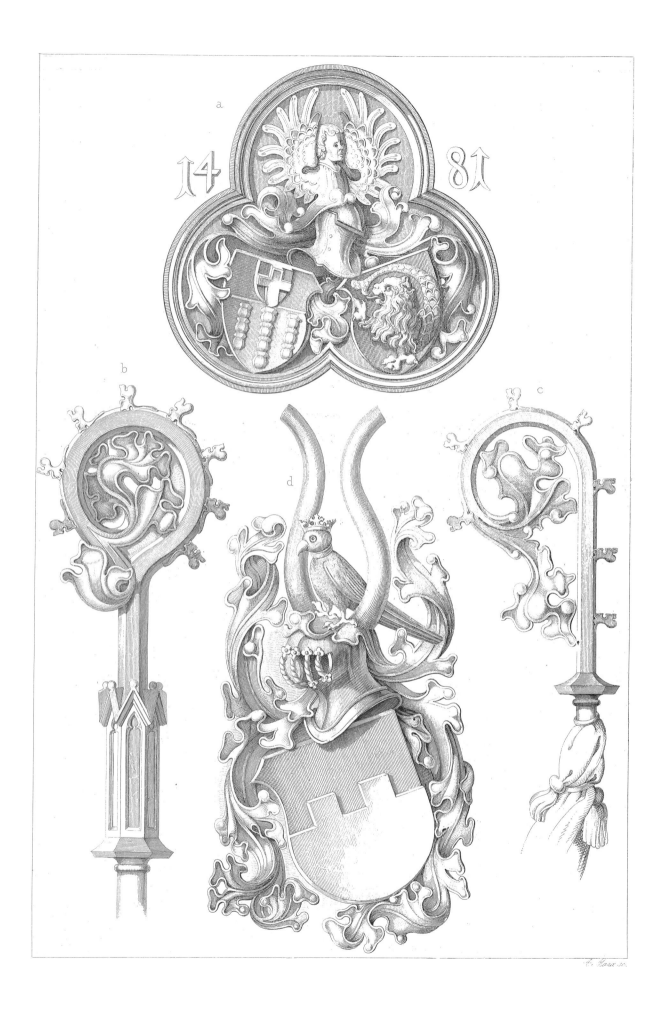

154. *a:* Carved wood joint coat of arms of the Nuremberg families Dill and Imhof. *b, c:* Late Gothic crosiers from a tomb in the Regensburg Cathedral. *d:* Coat of arms from the Regensburg Cathedral.

155. Wing of a Late Gothic altarpiece from the burial chapel of the noble family Truchsess of Neuhausen near Stuttgart.

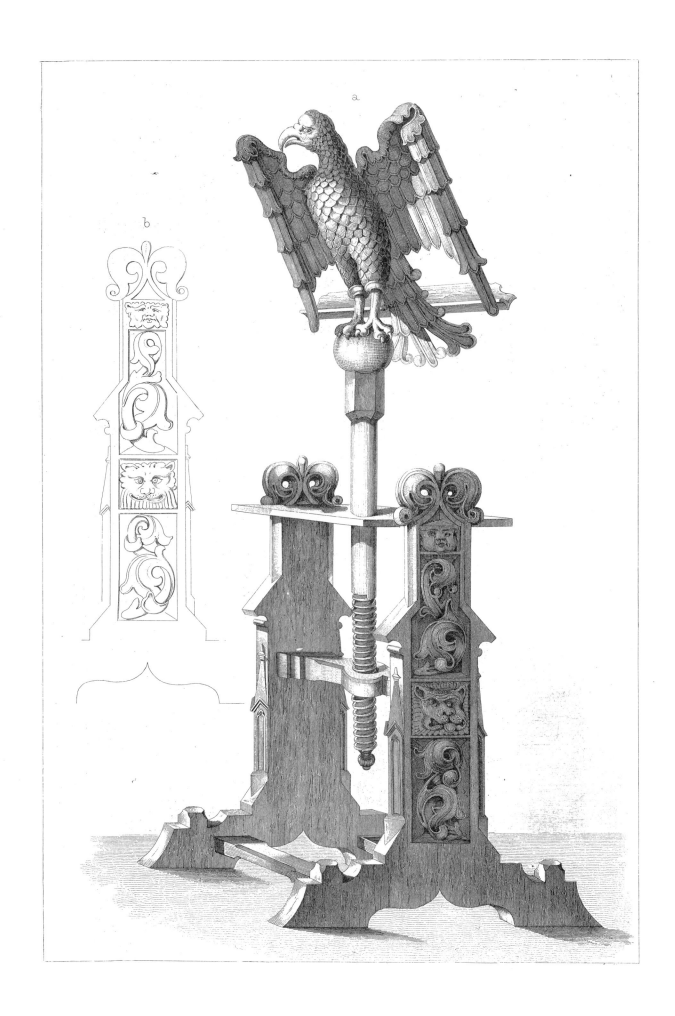

156. Late Gothic oak lectern from the collegiate church at Herrieden near Ansbach.

157. Late Gothic bronze chandelier from the church at Kraftshof near Nuremberg, with the coat of arms of the Kress family.

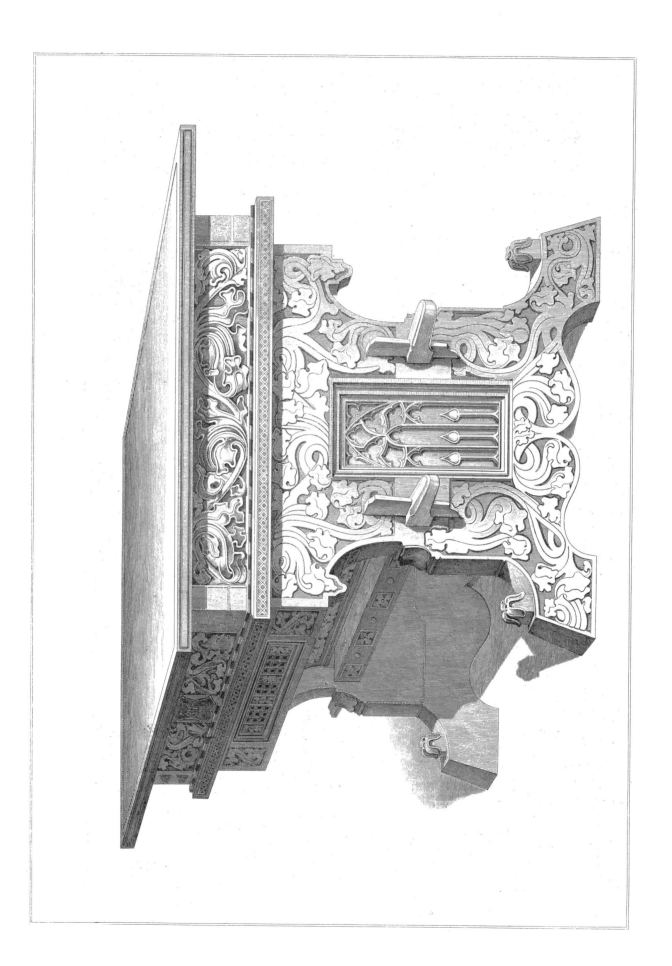

158. Late Gothic table from the former monastery at Kaisersheim near Donauwörth.

a

b

c

d

e

f   g

h

159. Details of the table depicted on Plate 158.

160. Late Gothic carved oak cabinet doors.

161. Romanesque portal from the church in the Cistercian monastery at Lilienfeld,
Lower Austria.

162. Restored depiction of a miniature on parchment from a French manuscript.

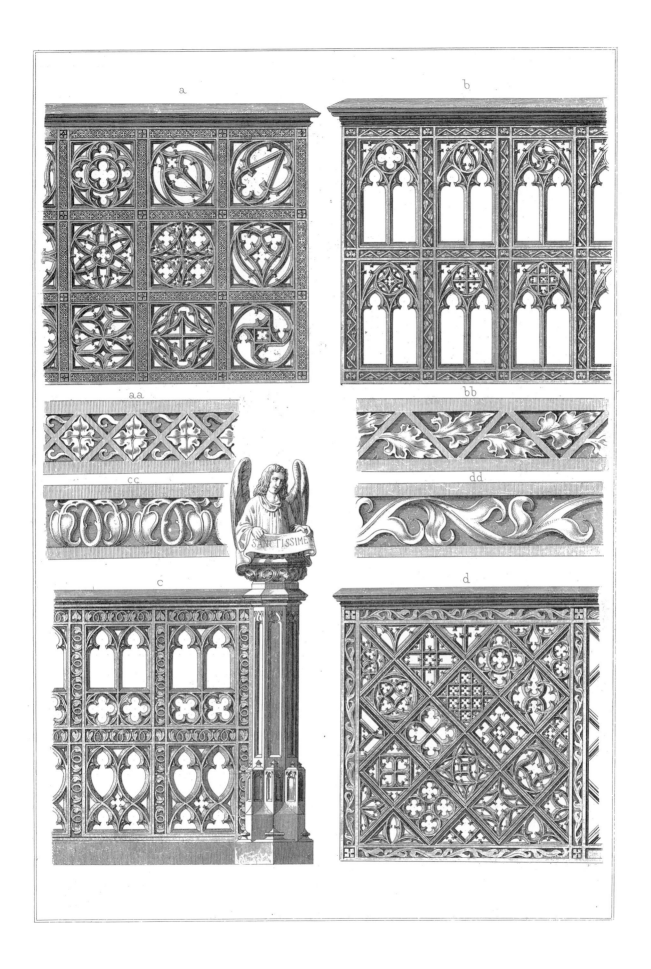

163. Painted and gilded wooden altar railings. *a, aa:* From the former convent at Löwenthal on Lake Constance. *b, bb:* From the monastery church at Blaubeuren. *c, cc:* From the monastery church at Laach, ca. 1480. *d, dd:* In the Church of the Cross, Coburg.

164. Late Gothic carved oak table from the parsonage at Hohenstaufen near Stuttgart, with the arms of the Wöllwarth family.

165. *a:* Late Gothic wall cabinet of 1480 from a private residence in Nuremberg. *b:* Late Gothic wooden ornament from the former monastery at Mönchsroth. *c:* Late Gothic wooden ornament from the monastery at Irrsee. *d:* Late Gothic ornament from the abbey at Tennenbach in the Breisgau. *e:* Console from the church at Owen, Württemberg. *f, g:* Console and frieze from the parish church at Oeffingen near Stuttgart.

166. Corner pillar of the funerary monument of the Pergenstorffer family, by Adam Kraft (died ca. 1508), in Our Lady's Church in Nuremberg.

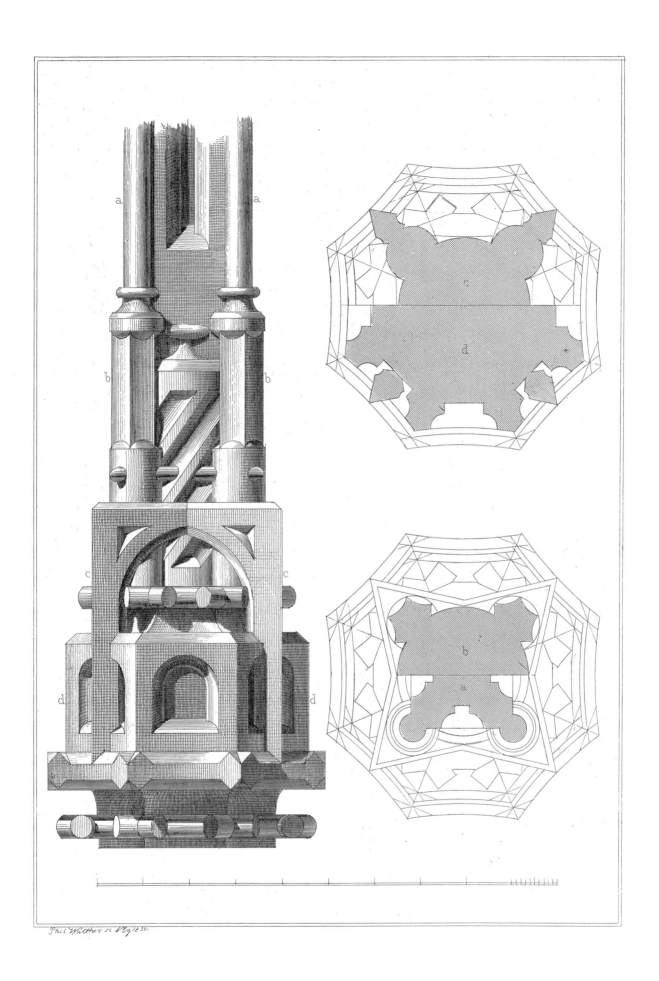

167. Another corner pillar of the monument in Plate 166.

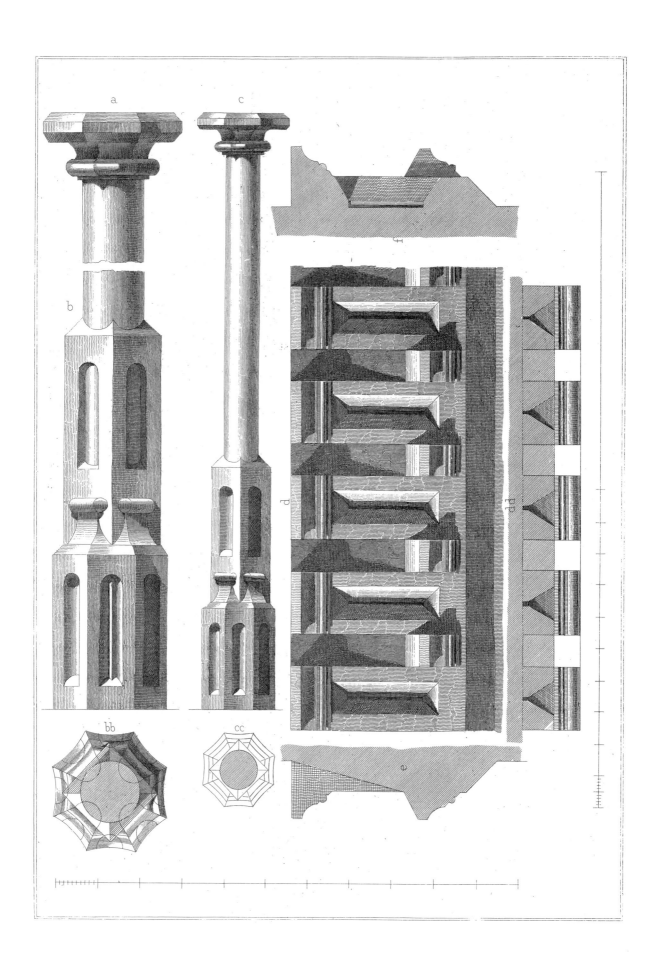

168. Details of the Gothic cabinet in the Augustinian monastery in Nuremberg.

169. Interior of the Romanesque Angels' or Peter's Choir in St. Sebald's, Nuremberg.

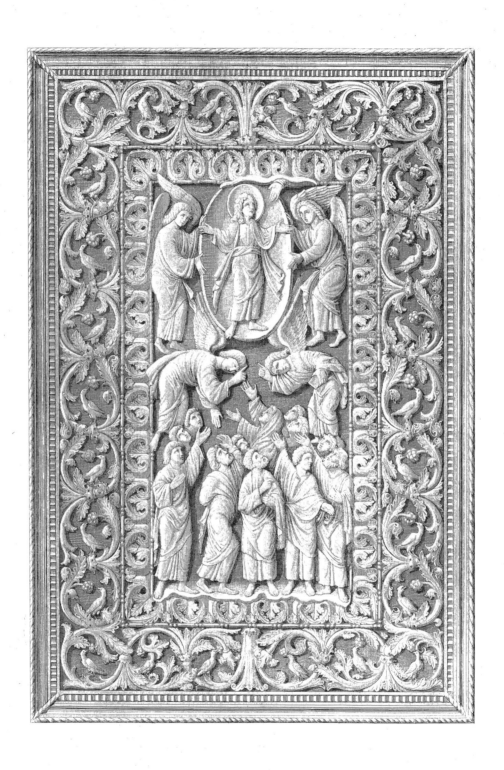

170. Ivory cover of a Gospel manuscript in the Ducal Library, Coburg, depicting the Ascension of Christ.

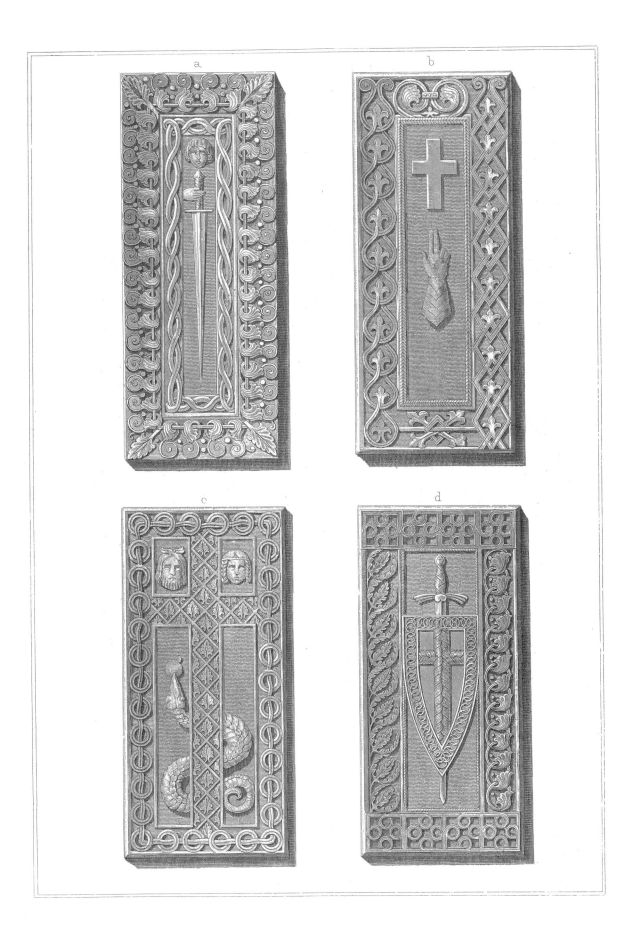

171. Gravestones. *a:* From the church at Welchingen. *b:* From Wimpfen im Thal.
c: From the former nunnery on the Rupertsberg near Bingen. *d:* From Laufen on
the Neckar.

172. Walls of a Late Gothic prie-dieu in the church at Kiedrich in the Rheingau.

173. Late Gothic door in the ruler's palace on the Veste Coburg, restored by Heideloff.

174. Late Gothic pew from the chapel of the Veste Coburg.

175. Late Gothic double goblet of gilt silver.

176. Late Gothic table.

177. Romanesque portal of the ruined Castle Krautheim, with Heideloff's imagined restorations.

178. Details of the portal depicted on Plate 177.

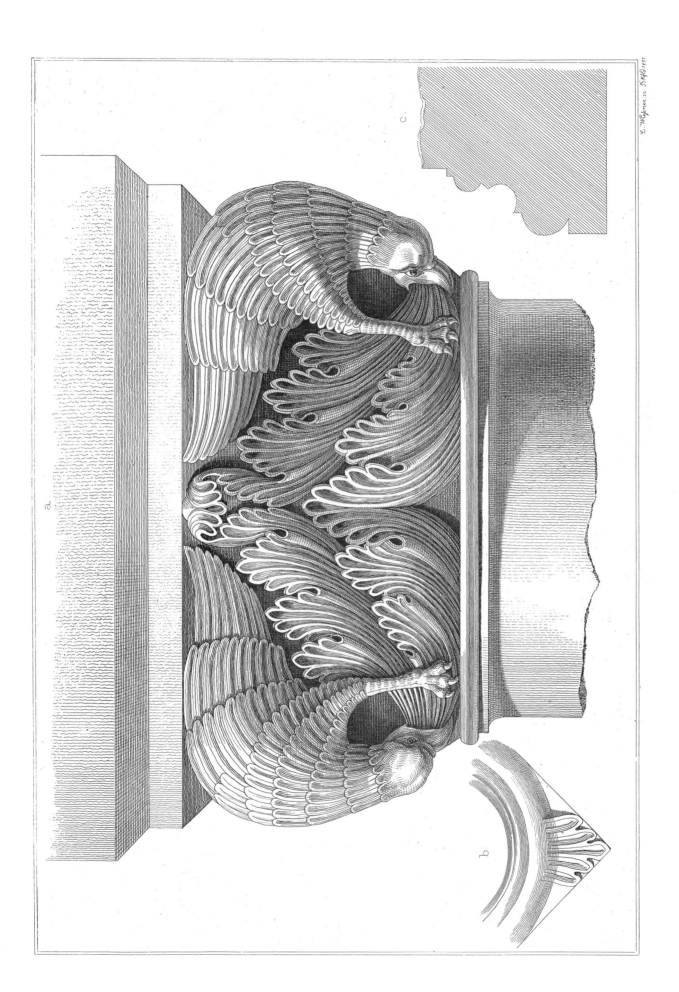

179. Romanesque column capital from the Wartburg near Eisenach, with a profile and a corner leaf of its base.

180. Vault consoles and capitals from the monastery at Lilienfeld near Vienna.

181. Vault consoles with figures of construction workers. *a–d:* From the chapel of the ruined Castle Landeck in Baden. *e:* From Falkenberg Palace in Silesia. *f:* From Friedick Palace in Upper Silesia.

182. Princes' or Rose Room on the Veste Coburg.

183. Early 16th-century painted and gilded ceiling in the knight's hall of the Bishop's Castle in Füssen.

184. Green-glazed tile stove in the castle at Füssen, dated 1514.

185. The St. Nicholas Chapel next to St. Lawrence's, Nuremberg, demolished 1851; Romanesque nave, Late Gothic choir.

186. Wall painting of the Virgin and Child in the Halberstadt Cathedral; imaginatively restored by Heideloff.

187. Romanesque capital and base from the so-called Landgrave's House on the Wartburg.

188. The Angelic Salutation, painting on glass.

189. Funerary monument of Count Hermann VIII of Henneberg and his wife, executed by Peter Vischer the Elder (1460–1529) after a 1513 design by Dürer; in the church at Römhild.

190. Funerary monument of Count Eitel Friedrich II von Hohenzollern and his wife, executed by Peter Vischer after a 1513 design by Dürer; in the city church of Hechingen.

191. Late Gothic doors from the Veste Coburg.

192. Neo-Gothic corner buffet designed for the Nuremberg citadel in a commission from King Maximilian I of Bavaria (reigned 1806–1825).

193. *a–g*: Details of the double chapel in the former castle at Rothenburg ob der Tauber. *a, b*: Windows. *c–e*: Principal cornice. *f*: Capital of the column in *a*. *g*: Detail of *b*. *h, i*: Enframements of similar windows in the Salzburg near Kissingen and Hohenzollern Castle.

194. *a:* Relief (restored in the drawing) from the double chapel in the former castle at Rothenburg ob der Tauber. *b, c:* Romanesque church candlesticks. *d–f:* Capitals from the ruined church at Reicherdsrodt near Rothenburg.

195. Romanesque tympana from the Magdeburg cathedral.

196. Lower part of the central window of the choir of St. Jacob's in Rothenburg ob der Tauber, donated in 1405 by Peter Nordheimer.

197. Princes' Hall in the city hall of Breslau.

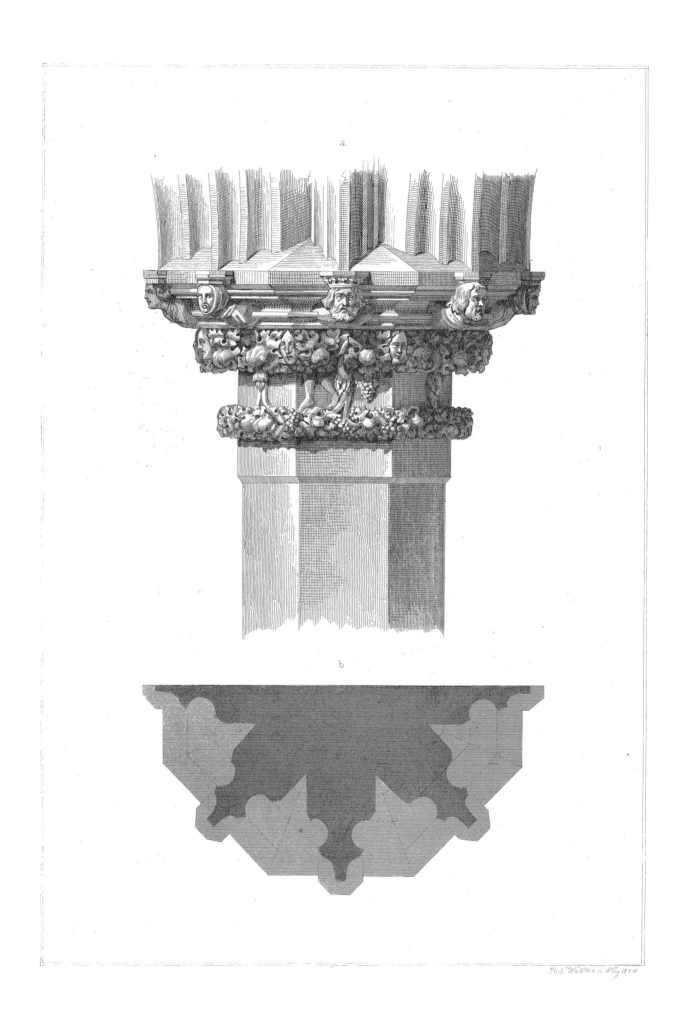

a

b

198. Details of the central pillar in the room depicted on Plate 197.

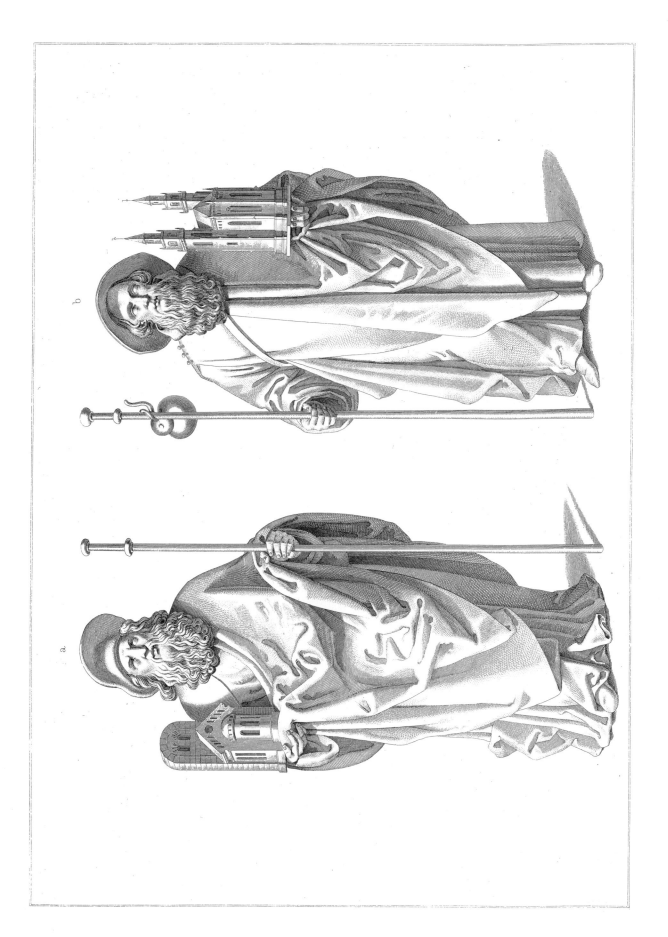

199. Statues of St. Sebald, patron saint of Nuremberg. *a*: On the west facade of St. Egidius', Nuremberg. *b*: On the altar of the Holy Cross Chapel at Schwäbisch Gmünd (wood).

200. Facade of the Wiss house in Nuremberg, designed and built by Heideloff.